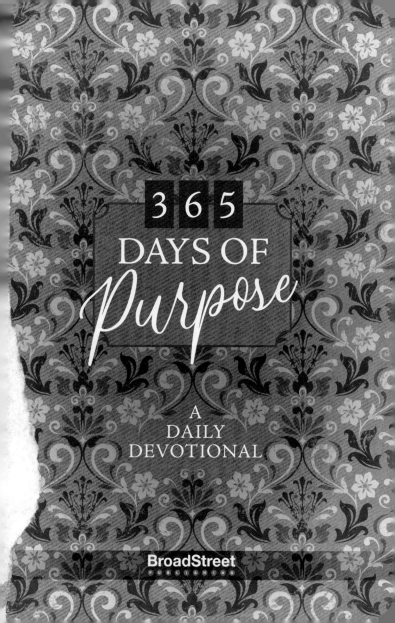

365
DAYS OF
Purpose

A
DAILY
DEVOTIONAL

BroadStreet
PUBLISHING

BroadStreet Publishing Group, LLC.
Savage, Minnesota, USA
Broadstreetpublishing.com

365 Days of Purpose

© 2025 by BroadStreet Publishing®

9781424568536
9781424568543 eBook

Devotional entries composed by Sara Perry.

Typesetting and design by Garborg Design Works | garborgdesign.com
Editorial services by Michelle Winger | literallyprecise.com and Natasha Marcellus.

Printed in China.

25 26 27 28 29 30 31 7 6 5 4 3 2 1

We are God's handiwork, created in
Christ Jesus to do good works, which
God prepared in advance for us to do.

EPHESIANS 2:10 NIV

Intro

God made you uniquely and specifically. Whether you've taken all the personality tests you can get your hands on, or you've just looked at the people around you, you will know that you are different. Different is good! God made you for a reason. He has a plan that goes beyond anything you could imagine for yourself.

As you read these devotions and Scriptures, be encouraged with hope! Meditate on God's promises that produce life and peace. Evaluate each day in the light of his truth and spend time getting to know his voice. Wait expectantly for him to reveal his plans and then walk confidently, knowing that he is always faithful and good.

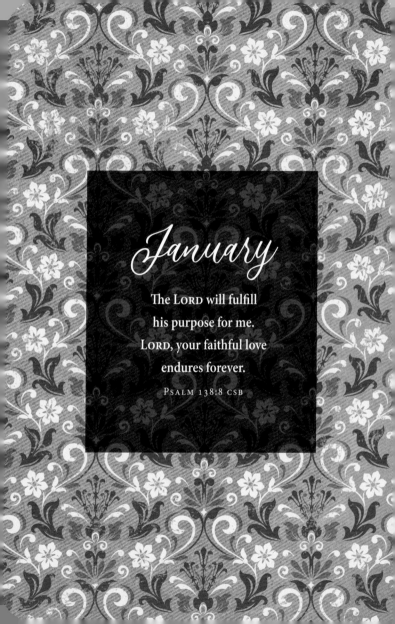

January

The LORD will fulfill
his purpose for me.
LORD, your faithful love
endures forever.

PSALM 138:8 CSB

Good Plans

> "For I know the plans I have for you," says the LORD.
> "They are plans for good and not for disaster,
> to give you a future and a hope."
>
> JEREMIAH 29:11 NLT

God's plans for his children are good. The paths we walk will not always be easy, but God's love remains steadfast through it all. He will be faithful on sunny days and when storms are raging. We can trust him to bless us with his goodness, even when we pass through dark valleys.

God created you with a purpose. He knows exactly what each of your days will look like, and he will fully equip you to walk through whatever they contain. He loves to strengthen you and build your character. God's intentions for you always stem from his merciful and kind nature. His love never changes, and his grace never fades. Lean into his loyal love and discover the goodness he has in store for you.

Spend some time asking God what his plans are for you.

All through Him

In him all things were created: things in heaven and on earth, visible and invisible, whether thrones or powers or rulers or authorities; all things have been created through him and for him.

COLOSSIANS 1:16 NIV

Everything was created through God and for him. Scripture tells us that God is love. Everything he does comes from love. This means that everything he made is filled with and surrounded by his perfect, unchanging love. It's woven into the very being of every living thing. We are full of life and blessed with goodness because of who our Creator is.

When you realize you were created through and for God, it can relieve the pressure of managing life on your own. Your purpose is to glorify him and find satisfaction in his presence. You can let go of the details and trust that he will guide you rightly. When you trust his sovereignty, you'll gain confidence in his ability to sow life-giving fruit into your life. Yield to his leadership and release your controlling grip on the path you take. You are his treasured creation; your existence glorifies him, and he is pleased with you.

Give God your anxieties and trust that as your Creator, he is in control.

There Is Time

For everything there is a season,
and a time for every matter under heaven.

ECCLESIASTES 3:1 ESV

Seasons shift, and circumstances change. No matter what our circumstances are, we can trust that God knows what he is doing. When we follow him, God will faithfully guide us into his goodness. He makes sure we are on the right path at the right time. We can move forward one step at a time, and trust God with details.

There's no need to compare your life to anyone around you. Your journey is unique, and God is in control! Though you may be tempted to judge your season of life by others in the same stage, that can easily lead to resentment. Throw off the need to measure your life by anyone else's standards and focus your attention on God. He is the one who knows you, sees you, and leads you.

Thank God for orchestrating your life and ask him to guide you through the season you are in.

Designed by God

A person may have many ideas concerning God's plan for his life, but only the designs of God's purpose will succeed in the end.

PROVERBS 19:21 TPT

It is not foolish to make plans or to prepare for the future. We were made in the image of the Creator, the one who builds and weaves everything together. He loves it when we follow in his footsteps. Still, wisdom is found in holding our ideas with an open hand. Despite our best planning, we must trust God to guide us through the turns and detours that we cannot foresee.

If you build your life on the foundation of God's wisdom, you will never go astray. You cannot control the future, but you can trust the one who sees the end from the beginning and every possibility in between. He knows your dreams and passions because he is the one who gave them to you. Don't take control of your life because you're afraid of how he might direct you. His plans are good, and he will lead you exactly where you need to go.

Invite God into plans you may have excluded him from in the past.

Inner Work

It is God who is at work in you,
both to desire and to work for His good pleasure.

PHILIPPIANS 2:13 NASB

God works within us with the power of his life-giving love.
He transforms us from the inside out. As we submit to his
leadership, he renews our hearts! He showers us with grace,
and he helps us live in a way that honors him. He empowers
us and equips us to persevere no matter what trials come
our way.

It is a gift to serve a God who is always close and involved.
He cares about the state of your heart. This isn't because he
is a tyrant who demands perfection. Rather, he is a loving
father who wants to see his children live abundantly. He
wants what's best for you and if you let him, he will gently
and consistently transform your life.

Daily invite God to do a deep work within your heart.

Generous Choices

Let each one give as he purposes in his heart, not grudgingly or of necessity; for God loves a cheerful giver.

2 CORINTHIANS 9:7 NKJV

God gives us the freedom to choose how we will give to others. He doesn't force us to do things his way. However, the more we look to God, the more we see how generous he is with us. He never withholds from those who need him. He provides for all, and he loves when we display his character by also being generous.

Generosity begins in the heart, and you can practice it by being aware of your thoughts. The way you think about others will impact how you behave toward them. As you hold others in high regard, your actions will begin to follow suit. Being a cheerful giver starts with loving others the way God generously loves you.

Find a way to behave generously toward others today.

For His Glory

The answer is, if you eat or drink,
or if you do anything,
do it all for the glory of God.

1 CORINTHIANS 10:31 NCV

We have the opportunity to glorify God in all we do. In big and small ways, we can lift his name high in our lives. In order to bring God glory through our daily lives, we have to know what pleases him. Scripture tells us that without faith it is impossible to please God. Faith in God's goodness, regardless of our circumstances, pushes us to live according to his wisdom.

There isn't one way to glorify God. You can worship him with everything you do. The way you eat, drink, work, love, and rest can be glorifying to him. If your actions come from a desire to please him, you'll surrender your life joyfully. Every moment of your day is an opportunity to have fellowship with his Spirit and follow his leadership.

What are you doing today for the glory of God?

Bottom Line

When all has been heard,
the conclusion of the matter is this:
fear God and keep his commands,
because this is for all humanity.

ECCLESIASTES 12:13 CSB

The instruction to fear God and keep his commands could be intimidating if we don't understand God's character or expectations. Without context it could sound authoritarian and rigid. Instead of feeling we can't possibly measure up to his standard, it's important remember that God's most important command is to love him and each other. He's not holding a list of requirements over our heads.

God is always gentle and kind. Don't get lost under the weight of performance and good behavior. There is no need to buckle under burdens that he does not expect you to carry. Lean into his embrace and remember that all he asks is for you to love those around you. When this is your highest aim, you won't be burdened by impossible expectations or laws you cannot keep. The bottom line of keeping God's commands is to love well.

*Think about how you can love others
in your interactions today.*

Brought In

God decided in advance to adopt us into his own family by bringing us to himself through Jesus Christ. This is what he wanted to do, and it gave him great pleasure.

EPHESIANS 1:5 NLT

At some point in our lives, we've all felt left out. It's difficult to be on the outside of something we want to be included in. The kingdom of God has a place for everyone. God has brought us into his family as sons and daughters. He has adopted us and given us a new name. He didn't do this out of obligation but out of love.

You can find incredible confidence in your position as God's child. You have a seat at the table and a permanent position in his kingdom. You are valued, loved, and chosen. You don't have to wonder if you belong or if someone better should take your place. You didn't sneak in or accidentally stumble into God's good graces. You were deliberately chosen, and you are thoroughly loved.

Meditate on what it means to be a beloved member of God's family.

Wise Living

Be very careful, then, how you live—
not as unwise but as wise,
making the most of every opportunity,
because the days are evil.

EPHESIANS 5:15-16 NIV

The admonition found in Ephesians doesn't come without the tools we need to accomplish it. God does not tell us to be wise while expecting us to figure it out on our own. He instructs us to live wisely, and he offers us an abundance of wisdom. He opens his hands and generously gives us everything we need to accomplish his will.

If you need wisdom, ask God for it. He does not hoard or refuse to share his abundant resources. He loves to give his children good gifts. If your desire is to honor his Word and live wisely, he will help you do it. You can confidently approach him and trust that he will not leave you wanting.

How can you embrace living wisely today?

Likeness of God

"Let us make man in our image,
after our likeness."

GENESIS 1:26 ESV

We were created in the image of God. Each of us reflects various aspects of his character. He made us with intention and purpose. There is not a single human alive who does not bear a resemblance to our Creator. As such, each person deserves to be treated with dignity and the utmost honor.

When you look at others with God's perspective, you'll begin to understand there is more connecting us than separating us from each other. No person is more beloved to God than any other. If you struggle to apply this truth in your daily life, ask God to soften your heart. Let him expand your capacity to love and open your eyes to the beauty that each person innately carries.

Ask God to help you see others the way he does today.

Wait for It

The vision is yet for the appointed time;
It hurries toward the goal and it will not fail.
Though it delays, wait for it;
For it will certainly come, it will not delay long.

HABAKKUK 2:3 NASB

All of creation moves in seasons and cycles. This is as true of people as it is of the earth. We set our goals and move toward them, but it is not always a linear track. Life rarely unfolds in a formulaic sequence. There are seasons of draught, rest, preparation, and even wilderness. It's important not to let these things discourage us from the vision God has given us.

Sometimes, your hopes may be delayed. This is not reason to give up. What God has set into motion will not go off-course. Even if you do not understand every circumstance, God is in control. Look to him and trust his timing and execution. Put your faith in his ability to see the whole picture even when you can only see part of it. He is reliable, and he will faithfully guide you.

Ask God for peace as you navigate seasons of waiting.

Experience His Glory

> "Bring me everyone who is called by my name,
> the ones I created to experience my glory."
>
> ISAIAH 43:7 TPT

When we come to Christ, offering him our yielded hearts, he gives us much more than we can imagine. He offers us forgiveness, freedom from shame, and fellowship with his Spirit. He gives us a new name, and he puts his mark of love on our lives. We run to him, and he shares his heart with us. We are meant to experience the glory of God.

God's plans for you are good. He created you in his image, calls you by name, and he wants you to experience his glory. He does not withhold good things from you. He is not waiting for you to get your act together, and he is not mad at you. You were made to dwell in God's presence and experience the abundant life he intended from the beginning.

Spend time in God's presence today, offering him your burdens and receiving his rejuvenating peace.

Already Known

"Before I formed you in the womb I knew you;
Before you were born I sanctified you;
I ordained you a prophet to the nations."

JEREMIAH 1:5 NKJV

God's Word says that he knew us before we were made. Before we were born, he consecrated us. We were created with intention and purpose. We've been knit together by love! We are God's precious creation, and he has declared everything he made to be good. He is happy with what he's done. He is not disappointed by us or dismayed by our failures.

God is delighted by you. He wants you to experience his love and know that you are adored. He has called you into his family, and you are free to experience the abundance of his grace. You were not made to stay stuck in cycles of fear, shame, or sin. God offers you new life and redemption. He created you in love, and he wants your life to be defined by that love as well.

How does knowing your origins change the way you live?

First Things First

"Seek first God's kingdom and what God wants.
Then all your other needs will be met as well."

MATTHEW 6:33 NCV

God is fully capable of taking care of us. This is why we can seek his kingdom with abandon and without anxiety. We don't have to be constantly aware of our own needs. We don't have to fret and wonder how we will be taken care of. We can put our energy into loving him and loving others, and we can remain fully confident that God will provide for us.

When your hearts greatest desire is to further God's kingdom, you can be confident that God sees you. He knows exactly where you might have a deficit, and he knows precisely what you need. If you are tired, he will give you rest. He does not ask you to give without assuring you that he will take care of you. You can rely on the abundance of his resources and the greatness of his generosity. Seek his ways, and you will be satisfied.

Choose one thing to do today
that puts God's kingdom and desires first.

Way Maker

This is what the LORD says—
who makes a way in the sea,
and a path through raging water.

ISAIAH 43:16 CSB

God is capable of handling every situation under the sun. There is no conflict, storm, tragedy, or sickness that is too great for him. His power does not have limits. His skills are not specific to one field of expertise. He is mighty, and he is worthy of our praise. He is the one who makes a way in the sea, and a path through raging waters. Whatever we are facing, he is able to make a way through it!

Wherever you find yourself, God is capable of leading you. He can guide you through the most barren wilderness, the most complicated maze, or the most disheartening situation. He will make a way for you through whatever barriers lay ahead. Trust him to do it. Look to him and follow in his steps. He has led people to freedom and redemption for generations, and he will do it in your life as well.

Look to the Lord when you feel lost and ask the Holy Spirit to show you what to do.

Always Good

God causes everything to work together for the good
of those who love God and are called according
to his purpose for them.

ROMANS 8:28 NLT

Not everything we go through in life is easy. Sometimes we experience inexplicable suffering, and sometimes we must navigate the consequences of our own decisions. Either way, Jesus never promised us a pain-free existence. Life can be excruciatingly painful, yet we can trust that all things will work together for our good. Even the darkest seasons of our lives can bring glory to God.

On your worst days, God is with you. He never leaves you or forsakes you. Though it may take time, one day you'll see how his goodness was woven through every season of your life. You are his beloved child, and he will not let a single one of your days go to waste. He notices every moment, every tear, and every situation. He orchestrates them all together beautifully in a way that is good for you. You can trust his ability to manage your life; he will not let you down.

Look for glimmers of God's goodness throughout your day.

More than Imaginable

To him who is able to do immeasurably
more than all we ask or imagine,
according to his power that is at work within us.

EPHESIANS 3:20 NIV

God is able to do far more than we can even imagine.
Our wildest dreams cannot compare to what God has in
store for those who follow him. There will be a day when
nothing holds us back from experiencing every good thing
that he has stored up for us. We will live in the glory of
his presence for eternity. We will be fully satisfied, and we
will experience the perfection that he intended from the
beginning.

God is continually working within you. As you surrender
your life to him, he keeps you on a path toward eternal
life. He is not finished with you. If there are parts of your
life that stir up feelings of disappointment or frustration,
don't be dismayed. You aren't out of time, and it isn't too
late. God knows the trajectory of your life, and he isn't
overwhelmed. As you follow him, trust that he will do more
than you can ask or imagine.

How can you see God at work in your life today?

Fixed Gaze

Let your eyes look directly forward,
and your gaze be straight before you.

PROVERBS 4:25 ESV

God has each of us on different paths. We all have different ways of navigating our lives. Keeping our eyes on what God has in front of us allows us to walk steadily and confidently. When we get distracted by the paths of others, we can lose sight of where we are going. We can't navigate our own lives well when we are focused on how everyone else is managing their lives.

Have you ever glanced at a distraction on the side of the road only to find your car start to drift in that direction? The same thing happens when you spend your life looking at everyone else's circumstances. Instead, let your gaze rest steadily on what God has given you. Manage your own situations well and with dignity. Faithfully tend to your own life rather than comparing yourself to everyone around you. Keep your eyes on the Lord and trust that he will help you every step of the way.

What is in front of you today?
How can you keep your gaze focused?

Wholehearted Reliance

Trust in the Lord completely,
and do not rely on your own opinions.
With all your heart rely on him to guide you,
and he will lead you in every decision you make.

PROVERBS 3:5 TPT

We can trust the Lord in every area of our lives. He sees details we cannot, and he knows how each day should be woven together. Though we face many challenges, God has solutions for all of them. We can confidently rely on his understanding over our own. While we may long to know the ins and outs of any given situation, we must faithfully surrender to the one who holds it all together.

You don't have to figure everything out on your own. There is great wisdom in leaning on God whose ways are greater than yours. When you rely on him wholeheartedly, you acknowledge that he is great, and his wisdom knows no bounds. If you ask him to, he will expertly lead you in every decision you make. Rely on him, and he will come through!

What situation do you need guidance in today?

Light of Truth

Your word is a lamp to my feet
And a light to my path.

PSALM 119:105 NASB

God's Word is not meant to confuse us. It is not a puzzle we must piece together or a riddle we need to decipher. Scripture is full of wisdom, and every part of it is intended to teach, encourage, and guide us. It gives light to our paths, and it shows us the next steps to take. We may not see the whole way, but we often have enough clarity to know the next right thing.

The Bible does not typically outline the nuances of every situation you face. There may not be direct answers to your questions, but there are always principles you are meant to embrace in every situation. You may not find a step-by-step formula for life, but you will find an abundance of encouragement and guidance. Spend time reading God's Word and let his light shine on your circumstances.

How can God's Word impact the decisions you make today?

God's People

"Once you had no identity as a people;
now you are God's people.
Once you received no mercy;
now you have received God's mercy."

1 Peter 2:10 NLT

Everyone who is part of God's family has a home. We share allegiance to his kingdom above all others. No matter which countries we come from or where we lay our heads at night, God has said that we are his. There is no ruler or authority on this earth who can remove us from God's care. We belong with him, and he is worthy of our devotion.

Your country of origin, ethnicity, social status, and wealth have nothing to do with your eligibility to be welcomed into God's kingdom. Even if you've never had a stable home, you can find a sense of belonging in God's presence. He doesn't call you based on your circumstances. He calls you his own because you are his beloved creation. No matter what shaped your identity in the past, now it is cemented in who you are as God's precious child.

How do your actions change
when you are assured that you belong?

Mindset Shift

Do not be shaped by this world;
instead be changed within by a new way of thinking.

ROMANS 12:2 NCV

Whether we like it or not, we are shaped by our influences. Our thoughts and actions are impacted by what we consume. This is true when it comes to media, entertainment, and relationships. This doesn't mean we should be stringent and legalistic about our habits. It does mean it is wise to be mindful and watchful. As followers of Christ, we walk in a great measure of freedom, but we are not meant to use that freedom to gratify our flesh.

Scripture is clear that you aren't supposed to live like the world. As a follower of Christ, you are meant to behave differently. If you want your actions to be different, you have to start with transforming your thoughts. Let the Word wash over you and change the way you think. As you fill your mind with truth, God will align your thoughts with his.

*How will you make changes
to any negative influences in your life?*

No Fear

There is no fear in love;
instead, perfect love drives out fear,
because fear involves punishment.

1 JOHN 4:18 CSB

When we experience fear, we are invited to know the perfect love of Christ. We are encouraged to surrender and let his goodness wash over us. He doesn't want us to be fearful or anxious. When we trust him to take care of us, there is no room for fear. God is love, and in him we find our home, place, and purpose. His love is unending, and we can rely on him wholeheartedly!

Think about areas of your life that are muddled with fear. What are you afraid of and how does fear impact the way you live? God does not consider your fear a failure, and he is not disappointed in you. Open your heart to him and let him show you how faithful and kind he is. Lay your fear, every detail of it, at his feet. You may be surprised by how tenderly he handles it.

Ask God to meet you in the places you experience fear.
He will show up with abundant loving kindness.

Strong Help

> "The LORD is my helper;
> I will not fear.
> What can man do to me?"
>
> HEBREWS 13:6 NKJV

God is our constant source of help. We don't have to wallow in fear when unexpected trouble comes our way or when we find ourselves incapable of handling a situation. God's strength is made perfect in our weakness, and he will always help us when we rely on him. In fact, when we are weak, we have the opportunity to glorify God even more. His glory is magnified when we admit our frailty and depend on his greatness.

God is never caught off-guard by the things that knock you off your feet. He fights for you when you are helpless, and he shows up every time you call on him. You can rely on him in every way possible. He is smart enough, strong enough, and big enough to handle any situation you face. There is no greater resource available to you. You cannot train, plan, or research your way out of a need for God. Rely on him for all the help you need.

Take your fears, worries, and burdens to the Lord today.

New Creation

We are God's masterpiece. He has created us anew
in Christ Jesus, so we can do the good things
he planned for us long ago.

EPHESIANS 2:10 NLT

God is steady in his opinion of us. We can't convince him
that we are ill-qualified or unwanted. We are his beloved
children, and he is filled with adoration for us. He created
us with intention and love. He doesn't look at us with
frustration or disdain. He sees us with mercy, and he longs
for us to know the depths of his love.

You are God's masterpiece. He created you, not only with
intention, but with absolute delight and creativity. There
is nothing within you that bothers him or causes him to
dislike you. He wants you to experience newness in Christ
so you can be near him forever. He wants you to find
freedom in the glory of his presence. He releases you from
the bondage of sin, and he invites you into the liberation of
his fellowship.

Today, remind yourself of the new creation you are in Christ.

It Will Happen

"Surely, as I have planned, so it will be,
and as I have purposed, so it will happen."

ISAIAH 14:24 NIV

God always follows through on his promises. He won't say something one day and then forget about it the next. He always remembers, and he will not overlook the details. When we are discouraged by waiting or unforeseen circumstances, God isn't absent. He isn't bound by the way we understand things. He is always present, always working, and always reliable. When we are discouraged, we can redirect our focus to the faithful one who always fulfills his vows.

If you are waiting on the Lord, be encouraged! Instead of being overcome by impatience, press into the fellowship of his presence. He is close to you even when you don't understand how his plans will unfold. Talk to him about your fears and doubts. He is not dismayed by your imperfect understanding, and he is not intimidated when your faith is weak. Lean on him as you wait and let him strengthen you.

Reflect on how God has been faithful in the past.
Be encouraged that he will be faithful again.

Forever Faithful

The counsel of the LORD stands forever,
the plans of his heart to all generations.

PSALM 33:11 ESV

God's plans cannot be thwarted. What he has purposed from the beginning will come to pass. This level of consistency should give us a great sense of security and safety. We can freely walk through our days knowing that God is in control. We are not powerful enough to intercept or ruin his plans. We are not capable of messing up so badly that he abandons us. His faithfulness cannot be interrupted by human folly.

Take a deep breath and steady your heart. Relax and trust in God's faithfulness. He will keep his promises. It's not your job to fulfill God's purposes. He may use you to accomplish his will, but he isn't reliant on you. The pressure is off. You are free to experience the goodness of his presence and the fullness of his love. His greatest desire is to have uninterrupted fellowship with you.

Rest in God's presence as you trust him to fulfill his purposes.

Build Trust

Perfect, absolute peace surrounds those whose
imaginations are consumed with you;
they confidently trust in you.

ISAIAH 26:3 TPT

It is no small thing to trust someone. It takes courage to be
vulnerable and allow someone else to see our weaknesses.
When trust is broken, it must be repaired and rebuilt
over time. Sometimes the breech is so painful that things
don't ever go back to the way they were. Our human
experience with trust is limited by our flaws, failures, and
disappointments. It takes practice not to translate those
experiences to the way we trust God.

Without realizing it, you might project your life experiences
onto your relationship with God. Have you struggled to
trust people and so struggle to trust God? This realization
shouldn't make you feel like you've failed. Instead, let God
tenderly heal the wounded parts of your heart. Take a
chance on him, and he will not let you down. Even if it feels
risky, ask him to show up in your life. He will meet you,
give you peace, and steadily your ability to trust will grow.

How can you trust God in a new way today?

Glorify God

"For this purpose I have raised you up,
that I may show My power in you,
and that My name may be declared in all the earth."

EXODUS 9:16 NKJV

Every person has a purpose. Our paths may look different from one another, but we all have the same calling. We are meant to glorify God and lift up his name. No matter the circumstances of our lives, we are all capable of fulfilling this goal. No matter what weaknesses we perceive in ourselves, they do not disqualify us. God is fully capable of using our weaknesses for something good.

You are fully capable of glorifying God. This isn't because of your incredible skills or your specific talents. Release yourself from satisfying a list of requirements. You bring glory to God's name by existing as his child. It's not nearly as complicated as you potentially make it. When you are convinced that you matter to God and that you belong in his family, your actions will flow from a place of love and acceptance.

When you feel insecure about your role in this world,
remember what God has said about you.

Blessings of Trust

Blessed is the man who trusts in the LORD,
And whose trust is the LORD.

JEREMIAH 17:7 NASB

We are blessed when we trust the Lord. When we trust him, we don't try to do things our own way. Instead, we rely on him for guidance, and we humbly submit to his will. Yet, even when we are stubborn or prideful he is gracious and full of mercy! Though we may waver in trust, God doesn't change his promises. We don't have to be perfect to know the faithfulness of God.

Scripture is clear that if you trust God, he will bless you. It isn't wrong to expect good gifts from your Father. This does not make you selfish, materialistic, or too focused on prosperity. You might run into trouble if you have overly specific expectations of what it means to be blessed, but you can't deny the blatancy of the Word. Trust God, and he will bless you. Ask him to strengthen your faith and show you the blessings in your life no matter what they look like.

How can you trust God more today than you did yesterday?

February

Whatever you do,
do everything for the glory of God.

1 Corinthians 10:31 csb

Set in Safety

You have not handed me over to my enemies
but have set me in a safe place.

PSALM 31:8 NCV

We can trust God to keep us safe. His presence is our
portion in every circumstance. God is with us on the
battlefields of life. He is our shield and our strength. Psalm
31 is a prayer of faith in troubled times. It was a song that
David penned in desperation. He needed the help of God to
save him from the plans of his enemy.

In one breath, David declared his thanks for God placing
him in safety. In the next, he lamented the misery he
was experiencing. Be encouraged! God can handle the
full range of your emotions. He is not put off by the
overwhelming feelings you have. No matter what you are
facing today, bring all of it to the Lord. He keeps you safe,
and he delivers your soul.

*Read through Psalm 31. Pray through the parts
that speak to your current situation.*

Abundance of Life

"A thief comes only to steal and kill and destroy. I have come so that they may have life and have it in abundance."

JOHN 10:10 CSB

Jesus made God's intentions very clear through his ministry. He did not come to judge or condemn people to lives of misery; he came to offer abundant life! He did not come to tear down, but to build up. He paved the way to God's presence and removed the barriers that had stood between God and people for generations.

In Jesus Christ, you have the opportunity to know the life-giving love of God. You have freedom from cycles of sin, fear, and shame. There is nothing standing in the way of you experiencing the joy of God's perfect presence. God is not waiting for you to approach him so he can condemn you. He is full of mercy and kindness, and he wants to refresh your heart.

How does your life display the abundance God intends for you?

Take Courage

"This is my command—be strong and courageous!
Do not be afraid or discouraged.
For the LORD your God is with you wherever you go."

JOSHUA 1:9 NLT

It takes courage to follow the lead of the Lord. This is because he leads us out of our comfort zone into the great unknown. We must trust his goodness and be convinced of his faithfulness. Even when we are unsure, we choose to step out in faith. We courageously depend on his guidance for our life.

Sometimes, life will be uncomfortable. In seasons of frustration, disappointment, or suffering, you can depend on the steady presence of God. Having control over the details of your life does not equate to success. Instead, success is found in having the freedom to trust God in every season. This requires having the courage to change, think differently, and follow God's lead. He is faithful through it all, and he is with you wherever we go.

In what area can you trade fear for courage and trust?

Resources

My God will meet all your needs according
to the riches of his glory in Christ Jesus.

PHILIPPIANS 4:19 NIV

In the midst of difficult circumstances, it's easy to forget
that we have access to the unlimited resources of our
Father. We worry and fret, wondering how we will possibly
get to the other side of our current affliction. The beautiful
thing is that we don't have to know. We don't have to fend
for ourselves. God is generous, and he is eager to give us
good gifts. He has more than enough to meet every need.

God does need anything from you. He doesn't need your
service or your resources. He just wants your thanks. He
wants you to follow his leadership and find satisfaction in
his presence. Instead of being overwhelmed by the needs
you see, partner with God's plans, and trust his provision.
We can trust him to do what we cannot. He won't leave us
hanging out to dry!

What needs are you trusting God for today?

Blessed beyond Belief

Whoever gives thought to the word will discover good,
and blessed is he who trusts in the LORD.

PROVERBS 16:20 ESV

When we devote ourselves to learning God's ways, we find goodness beyond our wildest dreams. He is better than any other! He does not manipulate us with his power or guilt-trip us into following him. He lovingly and kindly leads us to repentance. He draws us in with gentleness, and he fills us with hope.

Trust in the Lord and you will find freedom in his love. He will never forsake you, even when others do. He will never leave you to fend for yourself even when you keep making mistakes. He is a loyal helper and an incredibly generous Father. Great blessings are stored up for you when you put your trust in him.

How can you actively trust God today?

Gifts of Grace

Every believer has received grace gifts,
so use them to serve one another as faithful stewards
of the many-colored tapestry of God's grace.

1 PETER 4:10 TPT

We are all recipients of God's grace in unique ways. Every child of God receives from the bounty of his hands. It's easy to look around and wonder why certain people seem to have extra gifts or talents, but comparison only leads to discontent. It's important to see value in the way God made each of us. The things that differentiate us are beautiful!

There's no need to diminish your abilities or compare yourself to others. God has given you specific talents, and he asks you to be faithful in the way you use them. Ask him to reveal how he made you, and he will show you what he loves about you. Embrace who you are as his child and confidently use the gifts he's given you. You are needed, and the role you play in the body of Christ is important.

How can you be a good steward of what God has given you?

Give Leadership

Commit your works to the LORD,
And your plans will be established.

PROVERBS 16:3 NASB

Scripture encourages us to commit our ways to the Lord.
We are meant to acknowledge him in everything we do.
This means sharing our lives with him for the sake of
communion, acknowledging his consistent presence, asking
for help, and praising him for his wisdom. In each of these
ways we can include God in the details our days.

Today, confidently invite God into your day and trust
that he will show up. Thank him for the ways he has been
faithful to you and seek his wisdom when you are lost.
When you surrender your days to him, you can be assured
that he will lead you along the right path. Your plans will be
established when God is by your side.

Today, offer God leadership over all you do.

Wise Ways

There is a right time and a right way for everything,
yet people often have many troubles.

ECCLESIASTES 8:6 NCV

God knows the details that make up our lives. He knows
what each day will look like, and he knows what each
season will encompass. Everything is intricately woven
together with his wisdom and grace. When we submit to
his ways, he will keep us on the right path. He will lead us
faithfully, and he will show us the right timing and solution
for every situation. Even when we inevitably go astray, he
remains faithful and patient.

You don't know what the future holds, but God will always
tell you the next right thing. He loves to lead his children
through life. It doesn't matter how often you get it wrong;
every mistake is an opportunity to learn and embrace
growth. Lean into the love of God and he will help you
persevere through many troubles.

*Pause and ask God for direction
when you're unsure what to do.*

In the Morning

Cause me to hear Your lovingkindness in the morning,
For in You do I trust;
Cause me to know the way in which I should walk,
For I lift up my soul to You.

PSALM 143:8 NKJV

How we start our day can set the tone for the hours that follow. We may not know exactly what we will face, but we can certainly set intentions and prepare our hearts for what may come. When we start our day in the presence of God, we set ourselves up for success. We acknowledge what is truly important and we allow him to strengthen our spirits.

Every morning presents an opportunity to bask in the love of your Creator. Let him fill your soul and prepare you for your day. When you ask him for help, he will equip you to face whatever is coming your way. He will strengthen you and prepare you perfectly. When you yield your heart to God's leadership, he will guide you and keep you steady.

Listen for God's love in the morning
and stay open to his direction.

His Goodness

I am certain that I will see the LORD's goodness
in the land of the living.

PSALM 27:13 CSB

God's goodness is not a finite resource. It isn't limited in any
way! We don't have to worry about running out or fear that
we somehow missed receiving it. Each day we have unlimited
opportunities to experience God's goodness. If we pay
attention, we will see that he is always at work in our lives. He
has blessed us abundantly and we can only expect more.

David was sure of God's goodness, even on the dark nights
of his soul. He had many enemies throughout his life, but
God was with him through every hardship. Likewise, God
is your faithful help in times of trouble. He loves to give you
good gifts. No matter the circumstances of your life, you
can be sure that God has good things in store for you.

*Declare God's goodness over your life
with confident expectation.*

Taken Care Of

Give your burdens to the LORD,
and he will take care of you.
He will not permit the godly to slip and fall.

PSALM 55:22 NLT

God loves to take care of his children. We are never too old to depend on him! At any age, under any circumstance, we can give him our burdens. We don't have to carry them at all. We are not stronger or more mature for handling something on our own. We can lean into the complete provision of God and let him care for us. Maturity means setting side our pride and embracing our desperate need for God's help.

How often do you give God your worries? There is no transaction limit with him. You can give him each burden as it comes up. It is not holier to trudge through your days while trying to juggle everything with your own strength. Give him your burdens and let him refresh you from the inside out. He offers you rest and peace if you are willing to take it.

*Today, don't suffer under the weight of burdens
you aren't meant to carry.*

Overflowing Hope

May the God of hope fill you with all joy and peace
as you trust in him, so that you may overflow with hope
by the power of the Holy Spirit.

ROMANS 15:13 NIV

As we trust in God, he fills us with joy and peace. These are the riches that he generously bestows upon us. When we follow in his ways and surrender our lives to him, he meets us with abundant blessings. We are not promised wealth by worldly standards or the absence of suffering, but we are promised an overflowing portion of hope.

Hope will sustain you when the trials of life are too much to bear. Hope will feed your ability to persevere when logic is telling you to quit. As long as you have hope, you will remain faithfully committed to the Lord. The presence of hope in your life is more important than the details of your circumstances. No matter what your days look like, hope is what will carry you to the end.

Are you searching for godly riches or worldly riches?

Easy to Discover

He has done this so that every person would long for God,
feel their way to him, and find him—
for he is the God who is easy to discover!

ACTS 17:27 TPT

God longs for us to seek him. He knows that our home is
with him. We belong in his presence. It is the only place we
will find true satisfaction. We were created to seek him, to
find him, and to worship him. If he is not the object of our
affection, we will surely pour our admiration on something
or someone far less deserving. We will fill our time with
less worthy love while the Creator of the universe is steadily
calling out to us.

God is accessible to you. He is not far away or difficult to
find. His desire is for you to seek him, and he promises that
you will be satisfied when you do. A steady pursuit of the
Holy One is well worth your time and energy. There is no
greater task you could ever accomplish and no greater goal
you could ever set for yourself.

When you long for more than the world can offer,
remember that God is meant to be your greatest desire.

God First

Just as we have been approved by God to be entrusted
with the gospel, so we speak, not to please man,
but to please God who tests our hearts.

1 THESSALONIANS 2:4 ESV

We were not created to please man. We were not made to
bow down to each other or conversely put each other up
on pedestals. In the depths of our being we were made to
worship the Creator. Our words and actions are supposed to
glorify him. He is worthy of all our praise. When we speak,
we should not be worried about what other people think.
Instead, we should be more concerned with pleasing God.

If your main priority is to please others, you might start
to notice some specific symptoms pop up in your life.
You'll second guess what you've said. You'll ruminate
on conversations and anxiously wonder what everyone
thought about your words. This is not what God wants for
you. Submit your worries to him and let him gently remind
you how much he loves you. He is your highest authority,
and he is never harsh or unkind.

*When you seek to please God over man
how does your attitude change?*

Depend on Him

I will cry to God Most High,
To God who accomplishes all things for me.

PSALM 57:2 NASB

God can handle our problems. We don't need to filter our thoughts or prioritize our issues for him. We don't have to hide anything from him. We can approach him when we feel lost in darkness or full of shame. He welcomes us into his presence and pours undeserved grace over us. He covers our weaknesses with his strength, and he lifts us from despair into hope. He redeems every broken part of our lives, and he fills our days with his goodness.

No matter what you are facing today, God is with you. He is ready to help you and guide you along the right path. Cry out to him and invite him into your situation. He has not failed you yet, and he won't start now. When you cannot see a way forward, God knows what each step will look like. Trust him, for he is faithful!

*Declare today's verse over your heart
whenever you feel overwhelmed.*

Work All Together

In Him we have obtained an inheritance, being predestined
according to the purpose of Him who works all things
according to the counsel of His will, that we who first
trusted in Christ should be to the praise of His glory.

EPHESIANS 1:11 NKJV

In Christ, we have been given access to the Father. We are
heirs to God's kingdom because of what Jesus has done for
us. We depend on Jesus because we cannot work, strive, or
sacrifice our way into God's family. We need Jesus to make a
way for us. He is our righteousness, and we have come under
the banner of his love. He moves on our behalf, and he works
all things together for the good of those who love him.

There was once an impossible barrier between you and
God. Now, as you trust in Christ, you have obtained an
inheritance that cannot be shaken. There is nothing you can
do to earn a greater measure of Christ's favor. His death and
resurrection are more than sufficient for your salvation. You
cannot add to it or rely on your own work to be worthy of it.

Today, praise Jesus for securing your inheritance.

Through Every Trial

"When you pass through the waters, I will be with you.
When you cross rivers, you will not drown.
When you walk through fire, you will not be burned,
nor will the flames hurt you."

ISAIAH 43:2 NCV

If we could dictate our lives, we would probably leave out the parts that are uncomfortable or painful. We don't want to be overcome by the challenges life throws at us. Yet, when days are harder than we could have anticipated, God's presence never wavers. No matter what we are facing, he is near and able to help. His love surrounds us, and his wisdom is always available.

God's presence is your strength. This is true in every circumstance. Be bolstered by the fact that you are never alone. In addition, the one who is with you is stronger and more capable than you can imagine. There is nothing you can face that he cannot handle. He will uphold you every step of the way. God is with you, and you will not be overcome.

Memorize today's Scripture and let it be
deeply rooted in your heart.

United in Love

Make my joy complete by thinking the same way,
having the same love, united in spirit,
intent on one purpose.

PHILIPPIANS 2:2 CSB

The entire law is summed up in the command to love
God and love each other. The way we treat each other is
incredibly important to God. It matters more than our
accomplishments or goals. The New Testament is full of
admonitions of how we are supposed to relate to each other
as Christians. In Philippians we are reminded to pursue
unity in thought, love, spirit, and purpose.

Unity isn't easy to accomplish. It doesn't happen by
accident, and it takes diligence to maintain. You need God's
grace to set aside your differences and focus on what really
matters. It takes self-control to listen when you would
rather speak and use gentle words when you would rather
shout. If you depend on your own strength, you'll be more
likely to insist on your own way and opinion. You honor
God when you treat others with kindness and dignity,
putting their needs before your own.

How can you pursue unity with other believers today?

Step by Step

We can make our plans,
but the LORD determines our steps.

PROVERBS 16:9 NLT

Life is a balancing act. We do our best to make wise decisions, yet we know God is the one truly in control. This isn't to say our choices don't matter. God reveals what is best, and we get to experience the benefits or consequences of the path we choose. If we let him direct our steps, we can be sure to stay on the path that leads to eternal life.

Allowing God to guide you through life doesn't mean you won't experience pain or suffering. These things cannot be avoided, and they often produce good things in your life. If you follow him faithfully, you can be assured that he will direct your steps and keep you steady no matter what situations you face. He will uphold you when times are tough, and he will encourage you when you are weary.

Commit today's steps to the Lord.

Forever True

These three remain: faith, hope and love.
But the greatest of these is love.

1 Corinthians 13:13 NIV

So much becomes obsolete with time. Between generations there are vast differences in technology, culture, politics, and even the geography of our planet. Society changes and evolves for better or for worse. Very little in our lives is constant and reliable. When everything around us is changing at a pace we cannot keep up with, God's love remains. Above all else, we can trust his love to stay exactly the same.

If there is nothing else you can depend on, lean on God's love. It will never change or diminish. You were born to be loved by God and to reciprocate that love back to him. It is the most important purpose you have. Nothing else matters as much the relationship you have with God. His enduring love will carry you through every moment of your life.

Think about a time when God's love was steady
despite unsteady circumstances.

Mighty in Understanding

"Behold, God is mighty, and does not despise any;
he is mighty in strength of understanding."

JOB 36:5 ESV

Even the wisest among us cannot claim to know everything.
No one is an expert in all fields of study or knowledge. We
are limited by our humanity and our weaknesses. In order
to know the power of God, we must admit our own frailty.
We must come to terms with the fact that his ways are far
higher than our own. We are constantly learning, yet God's
knowledge is full and perfect.

Even though you lack understanding in many things, there
is nothing God does not know. By his Spirit, you have
access to his wisdom and understanding. You can go to him
anytime, anywhere, and he will generously offer the wisdom
you need. It takes humility to admit your weakness, but it is
always worth it to ask God for help.

*Instead of being discouraged by your lack of understanding,
lean on God's perfect wisdom.*

The Potter's Hands

Are you denying the right of the potter to make out of clay
whatever he wants? Doesn't the potter have the right to
make from the same lump of clay an elegant vase
or an ordinary pot?

ROMANS 9:21 TPT

God has steadily kept track of each life. Each person is a
unique creation. Each life has been formed according to his
purposes. As our Creator, he knows what is best for us and
how we should live. It is wise to seek to have his perspective
when it comes to the direction of our lives. Afterall, he
knows everything about us, and he sees us with love.

Your life is unique. No one else thinks or looks exactly
like you do. Your DNA is unique, and you were created
with intention and purpose. You are distinct in God's eyes.
He doesn't confuse you with anyone else. He knows your
strengths and weaknesses, and he knows what each of your
days will look like.

Do you believe you were created with love and a purpose?
Why or why not?

Fruit of Labor

The one who plants and the one who waters are one;
but each will receive his own reward
according to his own labor.

1 CORINTHIANS 3:8 NASB

We each have a unique purpose in the world. If we ask him to, God will steadily reveal it to us. While the details may differ, we are all called to do our work with diligence and determination. Though we focus on different tasks, our character should be in alignment with God's character. We are each accountable for our actions and should behave as such.

Your role probably looks different from your neighbor's. It doesn't do any good to compare the details of your life with everyone else. What matters most is how you approach the work God has given you. Work steadily and with humility. Seek to honor God with the way you handle your responsibilities. Commit each of your days to him and trust he will reward you for the work you do. Whether we see fruit on earth or in eternity, God does not overlook anything we offer to him.

Work wholeheartedly for the Lord today.

A Holy Calling

God saved us and called us to live a holy life. He did this,
not because we deserved it, but because that was his plan
from before the beginning of time—to show us his grace
through Christ Jesus.

2 TIMOTHY 1:9 NLT

God called each of us into his family. By his grace, we are
welcomed with love and kindness. There is nothing we can
do to earn his grace. He doesn't call us because we deserve
it but because we are his creation, and he wants to be close
to us. Our salvation is not based on what we can do but on
what God can do. He graciously offers redemption to all
who call upon him.

When you realize you cannot earn your place in God's
family, you can give up trying to prove yourself. Your
worth is already determined and set. As such, you are fully
equipped to live a holy life. You don't strive for salvation,
but you do strive to do the right thing in all situations. As a
result of being fully loved and accepted, you can confidently
live according to God's standards.

What is the heart behind your good works?

Do What Is Right

If you are mistreated when you do what is right, and you faithfully endure it, this is commendable before God. In fact, you were called to live this way, because Christ also suffered in your place, leaving you his example for you to follow.

1 Peter 2:20-21 TPT

Nobody enjoys consequences or punishment. It's especially frustrating to endure punishment when we didn't do anything wrong. As much as this feels wrong or unfair, Scripture is clear that it is an opportunity to honor Jesus. More than anyone else, Christ suffered when he didn't deserve it. In other words, he cleaned up messes he didn't create. He did this with honor and dignity. When we endure this type of injustice, we follow in the footsteps of Jesus.

Until Jesus returns, you will experience injustice on the earth. You will suffer when you shouldn't, and you may even bear the consequences for someone else's actions. Despite how painful it is, you display Godly character when you endure with patience and faithfulness. In times of injustice, call upon God to strengthen you. Lean on his strength, and he will uphold you.

When have you faithfully endured injustice?

All Things

I can do all things through Christ,
because he gives me strength.

PHILIPPIANS 4:13 NCV

God does not exist to grant us our every desire. We do not
follow him because he compliantly bends to our will or
gives us whatever we want. Our devotion to him is based on
his worthiness. When we read this Scripture in Philippians
and view it as permission to do whatever we want, we've
missed the point. Paul's reliance on God's strength came
from a desire to be content in every situation. He was
outlining the appropriate way to deal with suffering.

It is good to be encouraged by Scripture. It is also important
to understand the context of what you read. Paul was
expressing that no matter what situation he found himself
in, he could be content and continue to praise God. He was
encouraging the church by saying that his soul could be at
rest even in the worst of circumstances. When everyone
around you says that it is impossible to be content, you can
find contentment through the strength of Jesus.

*Declare today's Scripture over your life when it feels
impossible to find peace and contentment.*

Every Plan Fulfilled

"I declare the end from the beginning,
and from long ago what is not yet done,
saying: my plan will take place,
and I will do all my will."

ISAIAH 46:10 CSB

Though the world is a mess, we can be sure God is not. He does not feel overwhelmed or baffled by the state of things. He isn't pacing around wondering how everything became so out of order. He is not surprised by the level of deception, oppression, or selfishness he sees in the world. His promises will stand strong no matter how hopeless it seems. His plan will be fulfilled, and his declarations will come to pass.

God's faithfulness is your firm foundation. When you wholeheartedly believe he will keep his promises, you will be less likely to waver when trials come your way. You don't have to understand his timing or the details of what will happen in order to trust him. He knows what he is doing, and you can put your hope in him. He will accomplish his plans no matter what. He is the author of everything in existence, and you can rest knowing that every detail of your story is in his hands.

What is the fruit of trusting in God's promises?

Big Picture

Great and mighty God, whose name is the LORD Almighty,
great are your purposes and mighty are your deeds.

JEREMIAH 32:19 NIV

As we serve the Lord, it's easy to get caught up in our
purpose and calling. We want to please him and ensure that
our actions line up with his plans. It's good to evaluate our
trajectory, but it's important to remember that his purposes
matter more than ours. We aren't supposed to get lost in the
idea of fulfilling our individual calling. We are each part of a
larger story that encompasses all of creation. God's redemptive
plan is so much bigger than the path our lives take.

You fit into an intricately woven story. Lift your eyes and
look beyond the span of your own life. Recognize your
smallness and let it push you toward worship and adoration
of the Creator. When you can't seem to get your ducks in a
row, remember that everything he does is great. His deeds
are mighty, and he is worthy of your praise. Find solace in
knowing that he will accomplish everything he has set out
to do.

Align your purposes with God and you won't go astray.

March

I cry out to God Most High,
to God who fulfilles
his purpose for me.

PSALM 57:2 ESV

Chosen

"You did not choose me, but I chose you and appointed you so that you might go and bear fruit—fruit that will last—and so that whatever you ask in my name the Father will give you."

JOHN 15:16 NIV

One of the great mysteries of life is that God chose us as his own before we existed. Even as we choose to follow Christ, he reminds us that he called us first. Our surrender is a response to an invitation that has been there all along. How wonderful it is to know that his love has been with us through every stage of our being.

Scripture says that it is through kindness that God draws people to himself. When he chose you, he did it with kindness in his heart, not annoyance or indifference. He doesn't look at you with pity or obligation. Love and affection for his creation inform every choice he makes. As you follow him, you can learn to live the same way. With his love as your foundation, you can love others.

How can you display God's love to those around you today?

Heirs of the Promise

You are no longer a slave, but a son,
and if a son, then an heir through God.

GALATIANS 4:7 ESV

There is a wealth of resources available to us through God. The fellowship we have in Christ has made us heirs to an eternal kingdom. We don't put our trust in the rules or systems of the world. Instead, we patiently wait for the day that Christ will rule and reign. We are no longer a slave to our sins, but we are free to live the way God intends.

As an heir through God, you are given access to unthinkable riches and eternal glory. Everything God has is yours. He wants you to find full satisfaction in his presence. He wants you to be assured of his goodness and confident in his ability to care for you. You lack nothing because of the goodness of your Father and King.

What would it look like for you to live boldly
and confidently as an heir through God?

Fresh and New

If anyone is enfolded into Christ, he has become an
entirely new person. All that is related to the old order has
vanished. Behold, everything is fresh and new.

2 Corinthians 5:17 TPT

Nothing in your past disqualifies you from a full, rewarding
life in the future. No one is perfect. We all have struggles,
and we all carry various wounds and failures. This does not
mean there aren't opportunities for healing or for learning
a new way. In fact, God promises to make us new in Christ.
As we submit to him, we are continually being made new!

As long as you are living, there is hope for reconciliation.
You were made to be united with God in unhindered
fellowship. Is there an area of your life where you need the
freshness of a new start? God mercifully offers you what
you need. Ask him for help. He is in the business of making
all things new, including you!

Bring God the areas of your life where you feel stuck,
vulnerable, or disappointed. Let him bring renewal and healing.

Right to Receive

To all who believed him and accepted him,
he gave the right to become children of God.

JOHN 1:12 NLT

All who put their faith in Christ are ushered into the family of God. It is not an exclusive club where some are welcomed, and others are turned away. Anyone who comes to the Father through Christ is received with open arms. We are not held back by our sins, failures, ignorance, or limitations. When we reach out in faith, we are received in mercy.

When you surrendered your life to Jesus you became a child of God. This title cannot be taken away from you, and it isn't dependent on how you feel. There may be days you don't feel close to him, but the truth remains the same. You are his dearly beloved child. He is your kind and generous Father. He has welcomed you into his family, and he is happy you are his.

Do you believe that you belong in the family of God?
Why or why not?

Whose You Are

You are Christ's, and Christ is God's.

1 CORINTHIANS 3:23 NKJV

God has given us a clear outline of authority in our lives. Our allegiance is meant to be fully in Christ. We can certainly learn from human leaders, but we aren't meant to put our faith in them. No one is perfect, and when we elevate others, we set ourselves up for disappointment. We shouldn't hold any human to impossible standards. God is the only perfect one.

It doesn't matter how well known you are in the world. Whether you have a humble life or one that is on display for others, the most important thing is who you belong to. You have everything you need in Christ. He has fully equipped you to live in a way that honors him. The leadership of others is helpful and a blessing, but in Christ you are able to live rightly and fully.

Is your faith in Christ or in those you follow?

Trustworthy Strength

Some trust in chariots, others in horses,
but we trust the LORD our God.

PSALM 20:7 NCV

There is so much comfort in the presence of God. He is with his children every moment. There isn't a battle that we fight alone, nor is there a challenge we have to overcome with our own strength. Our hearts can rest confidently when we trust in the Lord more than anything or anyone else. Abundant wealth, political peace, or worldly success cannot provide the security that comes from trusting God.

Power, prestige, health, and wealth are all fleeting. Circumstances change and cannot be depended on. Sometimes you will face the consequences of your actions, and sometimes you will experience unexpected suffering for reasons you can't understand. The promise of God's faithfulness doesn't depend on you; it depends on him. Instead of trusting in your own strength, or your ability to control your life, lean into God's presence. Trust that he will accomplish what you cannot do on your own.

Where does your greatest sense of security come from?

Absolutely Nothing

I am persuaded that neither death nor life, nor angels nor rulers, nor things present nor things to come, nor powers, nor height nor depth, nor any other created thing will be able to separate us from the love of God that is in Christ Jesus our Lord.

ROMANS 8:38-39 CSB

What a relief it is to know that nothing can separate us from the love of God. Our busy schedules, greatest debts, and biggest mistakes cannot get in the way of God's love for his creation. Our lack of confidence or how others perceive us does not diminish the love of God in any way. Our inability to understand the depths of his love cannot change its existence! The reality is that his love is close, it is powerful, and it is our eternal sustenance.

The love of God liberates you from shame, fear, and regret. It allows you to find freedom in areas of your life that you cannot untangle on your own. His love motivates you to live in a way that honors him and to love others as he has loved you. Through Jesus, you have uninterrupted and unshakeable access to the greatest resource of all time.

Have you felt far from God's love?
How can you change your perspective?

Confident in Asking

We are confident that he hears us whenever we ask for anything that pleases him. And since we know he hears us when we make our requests, we also know that he will give us what we ask for.

1 JOHN 5:14-15 NLT

God is a good father. He listens to his children when they reach out to him, no matter the time. He is never too busy or distracted to listen to our prayers. He is available whenever we need him, both day and night. When we align our hearts with his, we will know what to pray for. When we pray for things that please him, he doesn't hesitate to provide them.

You can pray with confidence. He hears your requests, and he will faithfully meet your needs. If you ask for what is agreeable to his will, you can be sure that he will answer. Don't be intimidated by knowing God's will. It is clearly outlined in Scripture. God's will for your life is that you would remain in Christ. As you follow Jesus with a surrendered heart, you can be sure God hears every prayer!

Maintain an open line of prayer with God today.

You Belong

You Gentiles are no longer strangers and foreigners.
You are citizens along with all of God's holy people.
You are members of God's family.

EPHESIANS 2:19 NIV

When we come to Christ with our hearts open to receive his generous grace, he readily welcomes us into the family of God. His powerful redemption removes the weight of our sin, and it liberates us from cycles of shame. The light of his love touches everything in our lives.

There are no foreigners in God's family. We have all been welcomed equally as members of his household. Your background, language, ethnicity, or social status don't have any bearing on your belonging in the kingdom of God. Don't let anyone else make you feel like an outsider when it comes to your place in his family. He called you in, and it is his love that keeps you there. You belong, just as you are.

Why can you have a confident sense of belonging?

God's Home

Do you not know that your body is a temple of the
Holy Spirit within you, whom you have from God?
You are not your own, for you were bought with a price.
So glorify God in your body.

1 CORINTHIANS 6:19-20 ESV

In the Old Testament, the presence of God was isolated.
Moses encountered it in the burning bush in the desert. It
was found in the cloud by day and fire by night during the
exodus. Later, God placed his presence in the Ark of the
Covenant, which was put in the tabernacle. For hundreds of
years, God's presence could only be accessed by a select few.
However, when Christ rose from the dead, the Holy Spirit
was sent to every believer.

You have become the temple of the Holy Spirit. He
has made his home in you. This is almost too much to
comprehend. The God of the ages makes his home in
your heart. You don't have to worship a certain way or go
to a specific place to find God. There is nothing holding
you back from experiencing all that he has to offer. As
you surrender your heart to God, he blesses you with his
glorious presence.

*How do you find yourself searching for God
even though he is at home within you?*

Overflowing Joy

"My purpose for telling you these things is
so that the joy that I experience will fill your hearts
with overflowing gladness!"

JOHN 15:11 TPT

Jesus constantly taught his disciples how much he loved
them. He encouraged them to live in unity with him,
dwelling in the life-giving strength of his teachings. He gave
them a glimpse of who the Father was, and he showed them
the best way to live. In all that Jesus taught, there was one
motivating factor: the desire for his followers to share in his
unending joy!

Do you know the liberating delight of God's love that pours
over you? Following God is not meant to be a chore, but a
pleasure! Jesus wants to flood your heart with his joy as you
fellowship with the Holy Spirit. Spend time with him today
and experience the overflowing gladness that comes from
his presence.

*Can you remember a time you experienced overflowing
gladness? Jesus offers it to you today.*

Good Shepherd

The LORD is my shepherd,
I will not be in need.

PSALM 23:1 NASB

The Lord is our good shepherd. He leads us to peaceful places, and he restores his broken, lost, or tired followers. He meets our needs and ministers to our wounds. He is the who guides us through every twist and turn of life. We can always trust his steady hand. He will not lead us astray or forget us along the way.

The one who guides you is the one who called you. He knows your purpose better than you do. You can rely on his leadership, for he will never lose sight of your future. He sees the end from the beginning, and he leads you every step of the way. He does not overwork you or demand that you never stop. He leads you to rest, beloved.

Submit yourself to the good shepherd's leadership.

Willing and Able

"I know that You can do everything,
And that no purpose of Yours can be withheld from You."

JOB 42:2 NKJV

Nothing can keep God from faithfully doing all that he promised. His purposes cannot be hindered. He fulfills each of his promises with overwhelming mercy and unreserved grace! Especially in difficult seasons, we must remember that our limited perspective does not tell the whole story. There is more to life than what we can see or understand. This is why trusting God is so important.

Job provides an excellent example of trusting God through unimaginable trials. He didn't understand why God allowed him to suffer in the way he did, but he trusted him regardless. In the end, Job was humble before the Lord. He recognized his own weakness, and worshipped God for his strength. You can interact with God in the same way. Lay your burdens at his feet and remember that his ways are higher than yours. You can trust his faithfulness even when you don't understand.

Do you have inexplicable pain in your life?
Turn to God and rely on his promises.

Specially Selected

Stand up! I have chosen you to be my servant and my witness—you will tell people the things that you have seen and the things that I will show you. This is why I have come to you today.

ACTS 26:16 NCV

Today's verse outlines what Jesus said to Paul before he became one of his followers. Paul was still called Saul at this point. He was known for persecuting those who followed Jesus. He thought he was on the right path, allowing rage to fuel his pursuit. On the road to Damascus Jesus of Nazareth appeared to him and changed everything. He changed the course of his whole life!

God gave Paul a higher purpose and a greater destiny. He has done the same thing in your life. He changed your path and called you in a different direction. God reached out to you, and you responded in faith. As you surrender your life, you experience the goodness of fellowship with Christ. As you follow him, he will lead you into his loving light. What a gracious God he is!

How has God led you into your purpose
as you've followed him?

Good Requirements

Mankind, he has told each of you what is good
and what it is the LORD requires of you:
to act justly,
to love faithfulness,
and to walk humbly with your God.

MICAH 6:8 CSB

In this day and age, it is tempting to complicate the message
of Christ. It's hard to observe the nuance of being human
and resist judging each other in our best attempts to live a
God honoring life. When we simplify our expectations of
others and ourselves, it can better serve us as we seek to be
more like Jesus in this world.

Scripture brings beautiful clarity to what God expects of
you. He doesn't complicate it or make it difficult to attain.
Act justly, love faithfulness and walk humbly with God. If
these things are your gauge for success, you will never go
astray. As you find the freedom that comes with knowing
your life honors God, you can give others the gift of
freedom as well. Instead of overcomplicating his will for
your life, lean on what Scripture says.

*Which instruction from today's verse can you focus on
and implement today?*

Spiritual Abundance

All praise to God, the Father of our Lord Jesus Christ,
who has blessed us with every spiritual blessing in the
heavenly realms because we are united with Christ.

EPHESIANS 1:3 NLT

Every spiritual blessing is ours through Christ. Why would
we resist the goodness of God in order to say we lived on
our own terms? Being united with Christ doesn't mean that
we lose all of our autonomy. Yielding to Christ's leadership
means that we put his ways above our own, and we trust his
wisdom is better than our limited knowledge.

When you surrender your life to Jesus, you open the door
to all he offers. Through Christ, you have the ability to
have a life that is overflowing in the fruit of the Spirit.
Love, joy, peace, patience, kindness, goodness, self-control,
faithfulness, and gentleness are yours for the taking. As you
look to him and trust him, God will not hold anything back
from you.

Consider the spiritual blessings you have seen in your life.

Searched and Known

You have searched me, LORD,
and you know me.

PSALM 139:1 NIV

We were not created to be workhorses or robots. We weren't made to be measured by our performance. Though there are many spheres that will judge in this way, God never will. He loves you as much in your frailty and failures as he does in your strengths and triumphs. Though this truth is sometimes difficult to grasp, it is constant and unchanging!

In Psalm 139, we find King David's poetic song to the Lord about how wonderful it is to be known by him. God knows everything there is to know about you, too! He sees your heart, the questions you wrestle through, and the longings that lie deep within. He knows you intimately and loves you completely. Today, remember how completely seen, known, and loved you are. There is nothing better than being revived in the presence of God's affection and delight!

Spend time meditating on God's love for you.
Read through the rest of Psalm 139.

No Wasted Words

"It is the same with my word.
I send it out, and it always produces fruit.
It will accomplish all I want it to,
and it will prosper everywhere I send it."

ISAIAH 55:11 NLT

Scripture can be very poetic, painting pictures in our minds with the beautiful brush strokes of carefully chosen words. Isaiah 55 depicts the beauty of God's Word. It compares it to rain and snow watering the earth when it's needed most. Can you see how God's Word brings refreshing and new life just like a spring rain?

If you are thirsty and in need of new life, let your soul be saturated by the Word. Fill your heart with truth be refreshed by the power of God's promises. Soak up the knowledge of his character and let his instructions give you hope and freedom. Everything that God has spoken is meant to nourish, prepare, equip, and teach you.

Today, spend some time filling your heart and mind with God's Word.

Your God

As for me, I trust in You, Lord,
I say, "You are my God."

PSALM 31:14 NASB

Whether we surrendered to Christ at a young age or later in life, at some point we all had to make a deliberate choice to follow him. We must all count the cost and decide how we want to live. We cannot accidentally follow Jesus or stumble onto the right path. Somewhere along the way we must definitively declare that our faith is in God and our hope is in Jesus.

No one else can have faith for you. You cannot rely on the way your parents raised you, the faith of your spouse, or the decisions of people in your friend group. On your own, you must decide to humble your heart and submit your life to God. As you submit to his ways, he restores you and gives you a seat at his table. He welcomes you into his family and fills your heart with peace.

*Put your trust in God and remember
that his faithfulness spans generations.*

Partnership with God

I've done all this so that I would become God's partner
for the sake of the gospel.

1 CORINTHIANS 9:23 TPT

A clear vision can motivate us and keep us moving toward
our goals. Paul's life, as outlined in the New Testament, is a
great example of having a steady purpose. Everything Paul
did, from serving others to encouraging the church, he did
in order to partner with God and share the truth with those
around him.

What is your overarching purpose? What are the guiding
values of your life? What gifts has God given you
specifically? Gaining clarity can give you motivation and
perseverance when you come against trials. Knowing your
purpose can keep you steady when everything else feels
volatile or shaken. It can help you stay focused when the
path you are on seems confusing or rocky.

What can you do to bring clarity to your vision?

Complete in Christ

You also are complete through your union with Christ,
who is the head over every ruler and authority.

COLOSSIANS 2:10 NLT

All of us are searching for wholeness. We know that deep
down we are incomplete, and we long for true satisfaction.
Many people spend their whole life exhausting their
resources in a hunt for gratification. As humans, we all have
this in common. We were created to be one with God. He is
what we are all searching for. Thankfully, he has made a way
for us to find him! Jesus Christ is the only means we have to
be near to our Creator. His sacrifice is what paves the way
for us to experience the fullness of God's presence.

If you find yourself continually dissatisfied, it's worth asking
what you are searching for. Have you been spending your
time looking for instant gratification and easy fixes? Or are
you letting yourself be truly fulfilled by the soul satisfying
presence of God? He is not hiding from you. Through
Christ, he has made a way for you to experience every good
thing he has to offer. Yield to Christ, and you will find the
satisfaction your soul desires.

Let God satisfy your soul today.

All Things

"You are worthy, our Lord and God,
to receive glory and honor and power,
because you made all things.
Everything existed and was made,
because you wanted it."

REVELATION 4:11 NCV

God has done great things. He created the world, and he
holds it together perfectly. Nothing is a mystery to him.
We argue and debate over how things work, but he doesn't
have any questions. He knows exactly how many days the
earth has been circling the sun. He knows how and why
certain geological formations exist. He knows the name
of every single species whether we've discovered it or not.
Everything exists because he wanted it to.

You serve a powerful and wonderful Creator. He is worthy
of your praise. He fills your lungs with breath, and he keeps
your heart beating. Not only did he create you, but he
created you with love. He made you because he wanted to.
You are not arbitrary or accidental. Offer your praise to the
Creator and stand in awe of all he's done.

*Remember that God made you just as you are
with so much delight and purpose.*

Special Invitation

If you will carefully listen to me and keep my covenant, you will be my own possession out of all the peoples, although the whole earth is mine, and you will be my kingdom of priests and my holy nation.

EXODUS 19:5-6 CSB

God brought the Israelites out of captivity in Egypt. He led them into freedom in the desert. This is not where they would remain, but it was a step in the direction of their destiny. God invited them to be his own people—a people that would reflect his power and purpose to other nations. This invitation foreshadows how Jesus would invite all of humanity into the family of God.

Through Christ, God asks you to carefully listen to him and keep his covenant. He created a way for you to be free from the captivity of sin for all eternity. When you trust that Christ is your salvation, you step out of bondage and into freedom. While you may have seasons of desert wandering, each step you take after Jesus is a step toward your true home.

How can you listen to God and keep his covenant today?

Among Us

"The LORD your God is living among you.
He is a mighty savior.
He will take delight in you with gladness.
With his love, he will calm all your fears.
He will rejoice over you with joyful songs."

ZEPHANIAH 3:17 NLT

God wants to dwell with his people. From the beginning of time, he has desired communion with his creation. He longs to be with us. He wants us to know how much he loves us. Through Jesus, there are no longer any hindrances to experiencing the fullness of his presence. We are no longer separate, hopeless, or alone.

When you spend time with God do you experience his delight? Do you know how happy he is to be with you? He is a kind and generous father, and he loves it when his children turn their attention toward him. If you approach God with shame, fear, or insecurity, declare today's Scripture over yourself. God wants to delight in you, calm your fears, and rejoice over you.

Do you believe God wants to dwell with you?
Why or why not?

All Your Ways

In all your ways submit to him,
and he will make your paths straight.

PROVERBS 3:6 NIV

As Christians, we are meant to submit our lives to God. This means that we humble ourselves and willingly follow his instructions. Even when we don't understand, we trust that his ways are best. We can't say he is Lord of our lives while leaving him out of every decision we make. Our desire to honor him must be reflected by our actions and habits.

Follow God in every season of the soul. Every step you take in faith strengthens you and builds perseverance. When the path in front of you bends or seems difficult to navigate, you won't hesitate because you have a history of trusting God. The more you submit to him, the more natural it becomes. Faith in God is a habit you can build steadily throughout your life.

Practically, what does it mean to submit all your ways to God?

His Image

God created man in his own image,
in the image of God he created him;
male and female he created them.

GENESIS 1:27 ESV

God did not have to make us in his image. He could
have fashioned us in any way he wanted, yet we have the
privilege of reflecting who he is. As such, we should have
the utmost respect for his creation. Every human is worthy
of dignity and honor because each one of us is made in
God's image. There is not one person who is less valuable
than another. This is something that is easy to believe in
theory, but the execution of that belief is often tested.

As a follower of God, you are called to love what he loves.
The way you treat people, even in the smallest instances,
matters. It's easier to be selfish than to honor others, but
that doesn't line up with God's character. Ask him to soften
your heart and he will faithfully do it. If you are willing to
love others as he loves them, he will walk with you every
step of the way.

*What are some practical ways you can show honor
and dignity to those around you?*

Made Equal

All of you who were baptized into Christ have clothed yourselves with Christ. There is neither Jew nor Greek, there is neither slave nor free, there is neither male nor female; for you are all one in Christ Jesus.

GALATIANS 3:27-28 NASB

In Christ we are all equal. Through him, everyone has the same access to the Father. There is no social status, ethnicity, or standard of wealth that sets any person above another. We all have the same opportunity to humble ourselves before Jesus and receive a seat at the table. When we elevate our own importance above others, we've missed the point.

When you surrender yourself to Christ, you choose love, not only for God but for others. You choose compassion over competition, grace over jealousy, and sacrifice over self-protection. When or if the option arises, you choose to lift up your neighbor instead of yourself. By God's grace, you throw off the world's definition of worthiness and cling to what God says instead.

Choose compassion over competition
with those around you today.

Wonderful Depths

Look with wonder at the depth of the Father's marvelous love that he has lavished on us! He has called us and made us his very own beloved children.

1 JOHN 3:1 TPT

We are not meant to grow weary of God's love. Even if we experience it daily, we should expect to look at it with wonder. His love for us doesn't fade, and it doesn't grow cold. Though we are easily distracted and prone to wander, God's love is consistent and never changes. Despite our many failures, God has welcomed us into his family and called us his own. We are underserving of his miraculous love, yet he lavishes it upon us.

Do you stand in awe at what God has done for you? If you've been following him for a long time, it may feel as though your love has dwindled. If this is the case, remember it is never too late to rekindle the flame of your devotion. Remember his great faithfulness and look with wonder at the depths of his love.

Meditate on the depth of the Father's love for you today.

Always Kind

"Yes, I have loved you with an everlasting love;
Therefore with lovingkindness I have drawn you."

JEREMIAH 31:3 NKJV

God doesn't leave any doubt as to how he feels about us. Over and over again, he reveals the depths of his love. He has loved us from the start, and he will love us for all our days. If we pay attention, we will see that he is constantly showing us how much he cares. He draws us to his heart with kindness, and he showers us with mercy and grace.

God's voice always reflects his character. It is kind and full of love. When he calls you, he will not be contrary to his character. He is not angry with you, and he will not use harsh language. He will not berate you or belittle you. He draws you with kindness. He does not require you to change before you come to him. Instead, he welcomes you into his presence, and he walks alongside you as you seek to honor him.

When do you feel God's kindness toward you?

Out of Darkness

You are a chosen people, royal priests, a holy nation, a
people for God's own possession. You were chosen to tell
about the wonderful acts of God, who called you out of
darkness into his wonderful light.

1 Peter 2:9 NCV

Everyone has a unique story to tell. God has done
wonderful acts in each of our lives, and we can each testify
of his faithfulness in specific ways. We've all been liberated
from the shadows of shame and brought into his glorious
light. He has given us each a new name, and he has called
us to live according to his ways.

If you have followed God for a while, you might feel your
salvation less poignantly than you used to. Remember that
his work in your life is miraculous and wonderful. Reflect
on how God has been faithful to you. How has he brought
you out of darkness and into light? Instead of letting your
passion diminish with time, remember your true identity
and stand in awe of God's wonderful acts.

Today, glorify God and share a piece
of your testimony with someone.

Well Watered

The LORD will always lead you,
satisfy you in a parched land,
and strengthen your bones.
You will be like a watered garden
and like a spring whose water never runs dry.

ISAIAH 58:11 CSB

God is not threatened by our needs. He isn't discouraged by our weaknesses. Whether we lack physical stamina, emotional stability, or strength of faith, God is capable of providing for us. He lovingly leads us through deserts and seasons of famine. He is our sustenance and strength when we have nothing left. As we submit to him, he carries us through the trials of life.

If you want to be like a well-watered garden, you only have to keep relying on him. Listen to his voice and follow his wisdom. He is reliable and kind, faithful and true. There is no need to suffer through life alone. Lean on the Lord and let him strengthen you. Let him carry you through your worst days and rejoice with him on your best days.

Trust that God is your strength in every circumstance.

April

"Before I formed you in the womb
I knew you,
And before you were born
I consecrated you."

JEREMIAH 1:5 ESV

Faithful in Love

Those who know your name trust in you,
for you, O LORD, do not abandon those who search for you.

PSALM 9:10 NLT

God's faithfulness cannot be measured; it is greater than we can understand. As we look for evidence of it, we will see it time and time again! If we pay attention, we will see God working through the course of our entire lives. He is always present, and he is always moving. We trust in him, and he never fails to show up.

When you know God's name, you will trust his faithfulness. This is because the more you get to know him, the more assured you will be of his character. When you are sure of his character, you won't be swayed by the world's perception of who he is. You will be convinced of his goodness and confident in his promises. With that confidence as your foundation, you will call on him and expect that he will faithfully respond.

If you are doubting God's faithfulness,
spend some time learning about his character.

Valuable Role

You are the body of Christ,
and each one of you is a part of it.

1 Corinthians 12:27 niv

We each have a specific part to play in the body of Christ.
Each of us is meant to use our unique gifts to glorify God.
This is not meant to be intimidating. There is no pressure
to perform or obligation to fulfill a certain role. Instead,
we should hear God's Word and realize that we belong, are
wanted, and are irreplaceable. Every person adds value to
God's kingdom because of the intricate and deliberate way
he made them.

You possess specific skills and talents. Think about what
comes easily to you and let that guide you. You may not
fully understand your role yet, and that's okay. You have
space to explore and ask questions. Ask the Holy Spirit to
show you how God made you. As he reveals your gifts and
strengths, take time to invest in those areas.

*Consider how you can use your gifts and interests
to build up the body of Christ.*

All Accounted For

"Even the hairs of your head are all numbered. Fear not, therefore; you are of more value than many sparrows."

MATTHEW 10:30-31 ESV

God does not overlook small details. He is aware of everything that concerns his children, even things we deem insignificant. God watches over the sparrows, and he knows the number of hairs on each of our heads. If a sparrow cannot fall from its nest without him noticing, we can be sure that nothing in our lives goes unnoticed either. The Father cares deeply about the small details of our lives. He won't fail us when we rely on him. He is faithful to care for us as his beloved children.

If you find yourself filled with worry, let today's Scripture wash over you. If God knows the number of hairs on your head, he also knows each need you have. He will not overlook a single part of your life. You can trust him to take care of you; he invites you to rest in his faithfulness. Lay your worries, big and small, at his feet. He longs to give you peace and a sense of security.

Tell God your worries. Give him the exhaustive list and loosen your grasp as you trust in him.

Intimate Union

The one who joins himself to the Lord
is one spirit with Him.

1 CORINTHIANS 6:17 NASB

When we join our hearts to the Lord, we become intimately connected to him. It is far beyond a superficial relationship. We are of one spirit with him. The depths of his heart reach the deepest parts of our being. In this place of intimacy, we find a sense of belonging that cannot be replicated anywhere else. We were created to commune with our maker.

There is no need to hide parts of yourself from the Lord. He already knows you better than you realize. When you open your heart to him, you give him access to share his heart with you. You allow him to speak to the vulnerable places of your life. You welcome his input, not out of obligation but out of desire. God never forces himself on you. He is patient, kind, and understanding.

Take one small step of vulnerability in your relationship with the Lord today.

Divine Strength

Those who entwine their hearts with Yahweh
will experience divine strength.
They will rise up on soaring wings and fly like eagles, run
their races without growing weary,
and walk through life without giving up.

ISAIAH 40:31 TPT

Every person on earth has physical limitations. Our strength is finite and quantifiable. At some point, we will reach our limit. Even if we spend our entire lives accumulating power, we will still never compare to the strength of God. He is meant to be our true source. The strength he provides isn't defined by human ability. He empowers us through love and grace. He lifts up our inner man even when our bodies are frail and weak.

You don't have to strive for your place in his kingdom, and you don't have to work for your worth. You can depend on God to give you all the strength you need. As you entwine your heart with his, he will lift you up. He will encourage you when you are distraught, and he will secure you when you feel unsteady. He will renew you when you are weary, and he will give you perseverance when you want to quit.

*How have you been mustering up your own strength
instead of relying on God?*

Wonderfully Made

You formed my inward parts;
You covered me in my mother's womb.
I will praise You, for I am fearfully and wonderfully made;
Marvelous are Your works,
And that my soul knows very well.

PSALM 139:13-14 NKJV

God creates each of his children with purpose and creativity. He lovingly shapes our hands, toes, eyes, and noses. He kept each of us safe while we were in the womb, and he has sustained our lives since. God's hand has been upon us each of our days. We have never been without his faithfulness.

You were wonderfully made. Though it is tempting to focus on your flaws, your heart will become lighter as you turn our attention to the incredible way God made you. Your body, personality, and heart were all created with intention and skill. Have compassion for yourself. Try to see yourself the way God sees you. He does not harbor disdain or disgust for any part of you. You are a delight to God's heart.

Ask God to renew your thoughts and soften your opinion of your perceived flaws.

Good Inheritance

You belong to Christ, so you are Abraham's descendants.
You will inherit all of God's blessings because of the
promise God made to Abraham.

GALATIANS 3:29 NCV

All who belong to Christ have been grafted in as inheritors of the promises of God. As today's verse says, we are Abraham's descendants. We will inherit all of God's blessings because of the promise God made to him. If Christ is our Savior, and we have submitted our hearts to him, then we can be sure of the good inheritance that awaits us.

You don't have to do anything to earn your inheritance. It is a gift from your loving Father. You will partake in the promise because you belong to his family. You don't have to depend on your own status or success. He has declared that you are enough. Your position in his kingdom is secure because of his faithfulness.

Rest in the promises of God, knowing you cannot earn them.

What the Lord Sees

"Do not look at his appearance or his stature because I have rejected him. Humans do not see what the LORD sees, for humans see what is visible, but the LORD sees the heart."

1 SAMUEL 16:7 CSB

God looks beyond the façade of a person into their heart. He sees what no one else does. He recognizes what others miss. He is not swayed by charisma or clever lies. He is not surprised by our secrets or shocked by our sins. He sees us perfectly yet loves us fully. God never overlooks or misunderstands his children. We can rest assured that he sees every part of who we are.

When you choose to look past the outer appearance of others, refusing to judge them before you know them, you follow the lead of the Lord. It's easy to develop quick opinions. It's harder to take the time to really understand the people in your life. It takes time and deliberate effort to know people without bias. Despite the extra effort, remember that this is how God relates with you. Let him empower you to do the same. Allow him to open your eyes to the beauty that lies beyond the surface. There is more than meets the eye!

Can you think of someone you've written off without getting to know them?

Faith-filled Life

We live by believing and not by seeing.

2 CORINTHIANS 5:7 NLT

The Christian life is not based on what we can observe with our natural eyes. We are meant to look beyond the natural and focus on what is supernatural. We put our faith in Jesus, not because we can see him but because we trust firmly in God's promises. We hold fast to the truth because we believe that God will do what he says.

Let faith propel you to lay hold of the hope you have in Jesus. Remember that through Jesus, God will redeem all that is broken. Trusting in God's promises will give you perseverance when life doesn't look the way you want it to. When challenges arise, your faith will carry you through. If you feel weak in this area, ask God to strengthen you. He will build you up and equip you to walk steadily on the right path.

How does faith motivate you in your daily life?

You Are Valuable

"Look at the birds of the air: they neither sow nor reap nor gather into barns, and yet your heavenly Father feeds them. Are you not of more value than they?"

MATTHEW 6:26 ESV

At some point, we've all felt as though we are behind in life. It is discouraging to look around and see others living out the dreams we hope for. We must remember that God is with us right where we are. The idea of being ahead or behind is based solely on our perception. If we ask for God's perspective, we'll likely realize we are right where we're meant to be.

Don't worry about the details of your life. You can rely on God. He loves you so much, and he will never stop providing for you. His hand is upon your life, and he won't leave you to struggle on your own. Even when you don't understand the circumstances, God's promises never fail. He has not forgotten you. He will continue to take care of you every step of the way.

Remember how God has been faithful to you in the past and look with hope toward the future.

People of His Pasture

Know that the LORD is God.
It is he who made us, and we are his;
we are his people, the sheep of his pasture.

PSALM 100:3 NIV

In the days of King David, shepherds did not have an easy job. They kept watch over their flock, keeping an eye out for danger and defending them when necessary. The shepherd also cared for the wounded and weak. They were diligent watchmen and did whatever was needed to find even one lost sheep. Scripture often compares God to a shepherd. We are the people of his pasture, and he watches over us in the same way a shepherd cares for his flock.

No matter how wise or powerful you are, you have vulnerabilities. On your very best day, you need God to be your faithful shepherd. He watches over you with a level of diligence that you can't grasp. He sustains you, protects you, and guides you along the right path. His leadership is perfect, and his care for you is defined by gentleness and love.

*Do you recognize times in your life
when God protected you from harm?*

Embedded in the Vine

"I am the vine, you are the branches;
the one who remains in Me, and I in him bears much fruit,
for apart from Me you can do nothing."

JOHN 15:5 NASB

It is not the branch's job to bring nourishment from the roots to the rest of the plant. A branch is an offshoot of a healthy vine. Branches only produce fruit because they are connected to the vine. When we remain reliant upon the Lord, resting in his love, he causes fruit to sprout from our lives. We don't have to strive or work harder to make ourselves better branches. We are healthy and strong because he is healthy and strong.

Have you ever tried to grit your teeth and do better? It's nearly impossible to see results when you force yourself into actions or habits. Instead of despising yourself for not producing enough fruit, remember that true success comes from being connected to the Father. Remain in him and he will faithfully produce good things in your life. Trying to take control is a waste of your time and energy. It doesn't make sense, just like it doesn't make sense for a branch to exist without the vine.

*Remember that when you are connected to Jesus,
his life sustains you, nourishes you, and makes you grow.*

Empowering Love

Love empowers us to fulfill the law of the Anointed One
as we carry each other's troubles.

GALATIANS 6:2 TPT

Love allows us to walk together through trials. Love overcomes fear, and it overlooks offenses. It does not create shame, but it rejoices in the truth. Love is meant to be the foundation for all we do! In fact, when love is our motivation, we can be sure that God is the inspiration behind it.

Love is not just a feeling or a sentiment. It is the very nature of God. If you need strength to help others today, it is love that you are looking for. If you need patience to choose kindness over frustration, let love empower you. God's love enables you to connect to those around you and serve them well.

Look at your to-do list today.
How can love empower each of those tasks?

Children of the Light

You were once darkness, but now you are light in the Lord.
Walk as children of light.

EPHESIANS 5:8 NKJV

The world can feel like a dark place. There is much suffering, violence, fear, and shame. As children of God, we know that his light can shine no matter how dark and hopeless a situation seems. Just like the sun, the light of God shines on us and gives us strength. His light never fades, and we must remember to continually walk in it.

When you submit to God, his light shines on every corner of your life. He generously gives you all the grace you need. He equips you to follow him, and he showers you with mercy when you stumble or fall. You were once lost in your sin, but now you are not lacking in anything. You have his grace to make up for your weaknesses and his hand to guide you through each day.

What does it mean to walk in the light today?

Shine Bright

> "You are the light that gives light to the world.
> A city that is built on a hill cannot be hidden."
>
> MATTHEW 5:14 NCV

There is also nothing to hide in the light of God's love. Why would we try to dim in ourselves what God so freely offers us? There is so much grace, goodness, peace, joy, love, and hope in the light of God's mercy in our lives. We shouldn't try to hide any of it. It offers comfort to the suffering and hope to the despairing.

When we try to contort ourselves to others' expectations, we feel the pressure of what-ifs instead of the freedom of what is. We can live boldly, brightly, unashamedly in the fullness of God's love because that is what he wants for each of us. This doesn't always equal happy, satisfied, and it certainly doesn't mean perfect. But light clears up what was unclear in the fog of confusion and trying to figure out how to please everyone around us. Light doesn't change what it is. We have to know who we are, how incredibly beloved we are, and then we will know the power there lies in simply being ourselves, in the fullness of God's mercy-kindness!

Focus less on what others may think of you
and more on living in the freedom of God's love today.

Power of Faith

Through faith you are all sons of God in Christ Jesus.

GALATIANS 3:26 CSB

Through Christ, we are children of God. We are not stepchildren or orphans. We are not treated as second-class citizens or foreigners in a land we don't belong to. By faith, we become heirs to the throne and are grafted into God's family. Faith moves us from being outsiders to insiders. The invitation to be part of God's family is open all who will come to Christ with humility.

Jesus' death and resurrection gives you the right to be called a child of God. When you acknowledge what he has done for you, you become part of God's family. Your position has nothing to do with your strengths or weaknesses. Instead, it is fully dependent on the sacrifice of Jesus. He has made a way for you to have belonging and security for all eternity.

How can you grow in faith today?

Persistent Peace

May the Lord of peace himself give you his peace at all times and in every situation. The Lord be with you all.

2 Thessalonians 3:16 NLT

The peace of God is persistent and always available. It is like an ever-flowing fountain we can draw from in our time of need. When God is with us, we have the peace of his presence. As we turn our attention to the one who never leaves us, we will be strengthened and reassured of his goodness. His nearness is one of our greatest blessings.

The peace of God isn't a fleeting feeling. It isn't just an inkling that maybe everything will be okay. God's peace is the assurance of his faithfulness. It is found in knowing without a doubt that he will be true to his Word. His peace is available at all times and in every situation. It isn't something you muster up or force yourself to believe. God's peace is a gift that he gives freely and generously. No matter what you face today, God is with you.

Take time to enjoy the peace of God's presence today.

Rely on Love

We know and rely on the love God has for us. God is love.
Whoever lives in love lives in God, and God in them.

1 JOHN 4:16 NIV

If we wholeheartedly love God and others, we honor God's desire for his creation. We were created to experience the fullness of his love and to share that love with those around us. The expression of his love through us indicates that we belong to him. Love is what separates us from the world. It defines who we are, and it declares who we belong to.

What does it mean to rely on God's love? When you trust in the work of Christ over your own striving, you rely on God's love. When you believe that God will keep his promises no matter the circumstances you face, you rely on God's love. Each day that you acknowledge his ways and submit your will to his plans, you rely on God's love.

How has God's love impacted your life?

Poetic Truth

"'In him we live and move and have our being';
as even some of your own poets have said,
"'For we are indeed his offspring.'"

ACTS 17:28 ESV

We are the living poetry of God. He dreamed us up, knit us together, and breathed life into our souls. Our entire being is founded and sustained in the heart of God. We are his children, and he finds delight in us. He longs for each of us to find our home in his presence. Everything he has done stems from his desire to have unhindered fellowship with his creation.

You are a work of art and piece of God's favorite prose. You are an expression of his love and a reflection of his image. When he created you, he paid attention to each part. He finely tuned and crafted you. Success or wealth are not what make your life meaningful. You have innate value because of who your Creator is. Your existence glorifies him and is evidence of his loving kindness.

*How does God's delight in you impact
how you approach your purpose?*

Unnecessary Burdens

Do not be anxious about anything,
but in everything by prayer and pleading with thanksgiving
let your requests be made known to God.

PHILIPPIANS 4:6 NASB

God's faithfulness is our foundation. Even though we have many weaknesses and limitations, we can stand firmly by relying on his power. We can bring God all our worries, cares, fears, and needs. As we offer them to him through prayer, we acknowledge that we need his help in everything we do. Prayer is an act of humility. Giving him our burdens is a declaration that we cannot handle them on our own.

Instead of worrying about everything you cannot control, create a ritual of handing your burdens to God. Let prayer, pleading, and thanksgiving be a quick reflex in your life. When worry comes knocking, don't even give it a second thought. Hand your anxiety to God like someone who received their neighbors mail on accident. It doesn't have to be a big drawn-out process. Simply refuse to carry burdens that God is offering to help you with.

Have you let anxiety control your life?
Give your burdens to God.

Deep Well

A man of deep understanding will
give good advice,
drawing it out from the well within.

PROVERBS 20:5 TPT

It is incredibly valuable to know wise counselors and friends. They can help us shift perspective from our limited view to a place of deeper understanding. Leaning on the understanding of others is a precious gift because we cannot navigate life alone. We need the input, guidance, and viewpoint of others. We each have something valuable to offer the body, and we all benefit when we acknowledge the wisdom each other has.

If you have a friend who gives good advice, founded on the wisdom of God, you are richly blessed. If you feel like an island, make every effort to surround yourself with people who embrace understanding and continuously seek to grow in their knowledge of God. Their desire to have a deep well of wisdom in their own lives will only benefit you as you seek to honor God in all you do.

Actively seek the wisdom of others today.

Transformative Work

The LORD will perfect that which concerns me;
Your mercy, O LORD, endures forever;
Do not forsake the works of Your hands.

PSALM 138:8 NKJV

As we surrender to him, God transforms us. He redeems
what is lost, and he fixes what is broken. He guides us
through our days, and we bear fruit as we spend time in
his presence. There aren't any areas of our lives that are
off-limits to his goodness. The more he transforms us from
within, the more our choices and interactions reflect his
character.

God is a promise keeper. If he says he will do something,
you can trust him to do it. He finishes every good work he
starts. Your life is the work of his hands. From the moment
of your conception, God began a specific and beautiful
work in you. He won't stop until his love has perfected your
life. As long as you live, your loving Father is working in
and around you.

*You are a work in process, and you can trust God
to do what he does best.*

Always Faithful

"I will make what I have said come true;
I will do what I have planned."

ISAIAH 46:11 NCV

God will follow through on every purpose and plan he
set into place. He keeps his word without exception.
His ability to fulfill his promises doesn't depend on our
abilities, success, or failures. His Word is dependent on his
faithfulness and the strength of his character. He is without
fault, so we can rely on everything he says. He has no
reason to lie, manipulate, or stretch the truth.

God is purposeful. Everything he does lines up with his
end goal. He is never distracted or derailed. There may be
times in your life when you drift off course. You might even
wander away deliberately. Even so, God's purposes remain.
You can always come back to him. He remains steady and
unchanging even when you are not. He is faithful and true
even when you are full of doubt.

Is your confidence in God's faithfulness or in your own abilities?

Taste and See

Taste and see that the LORD is good.
How happy is the person who takes refuge in him!

PSALM 34:8 CSB

We have all received the same invitation to taste and
see that the Lord is good. He calls out to us and gives us
permission to experience his goodness. It is our job to
respond to his offer. We were made to worship him and
to seek his face. When we devote our lives to this, we will
surely know that he is good.

Today is full of opportunities to taste and see the goodness
of God. He has filled the earth with his glory, and he is not
hiding from you. Everywhere you look there are glimpses of
his goodness. The more you spend time with him, the more
you will begin to see his work all around you. Run to him
and receive what he offers with thanksgiving and joy.

How have you experienced the goodness of God lately?

Trust the Lord

Greed causes fighting;
trusting the LORD leads to prosperity.
Those who trust their own insight are foolish,
but anyone who walks in wisdom is safe.

PROVERBS 28:25-26 NLT

We don't need to seek prosperity for ourselves. When we trust God, he promises to provide for us. He generously blesses us with his presence, and he mercifully gives us eternal security for our souls. It is nonsensical to think our plans are better than his or that our needs will only be met by our own striving. Instead, we show we are wise when we lean on his understanding. Trusting God means we don't need to frantically search for blessings and wealth.

God knows what you need. He knows what each day will hold, and he knows how to equip you to handle it. When you humbly admit to your weaknesses, you make room for God to be sovereign in your life. From that place, you can follow God without barriers or inhibitions. Your humility allows God to transform your understanding and meet you where you are. Trust him and he will lead you to prosperity.

*How do you trust the Lord more than
your own insights and ideas?*

Great Love

"If you, imperfect as you are, know how to lovingly take care of your children and give them what's best, how much more ready is your heavenly Father to give wonderful gifts to those who ask him?"

MATTHEW 7:11 TPT

Though we are imperfect, we still know how to treat others with kindness and respect. Our definitions may differ, but we typically have some idea of how to care for each other. Despite our great weaknesses and the limitations of our humanity, we love each other the best we can. If our feeble attempts at love count, imagine how perfect God's love is. He loves us without limitations or weaknesses.

God's love for you is perfect, and he loves to give you wonderful gifts. No matter what your experience with people has been, God's love is always good. It is whole, pure, and without fault. His love is not dependent on your ability to earn it or receive it. His love for you is steady, unshakeable, and unending. He knows what is best for you, and he wants you to experience all he has to offer.

Consider the most loving relationship in your life and how God's love is even greater.

Firm Foundation

Let love be genuine. Abhor what is evil;
hold fast to what is good.

ROMANS 12:9 ESV

God calls us to hate evil and to love what is good. This is
difficult to do if we are unfamiliar with how to define those
things. The only way for us to navigate the world around
us is to start with a firm foundation of the truth. We can
measure everything we see against God's character. In order
to know God's character, we must spend time with him and
fill our hearts with the power of his Word.

If you want your love to be genuine, you must first receive
genuine love from the source. If you want to hate evil and
love what is good, you must thoroughly know the truth.
Both things require you to seek the presence of God. When
you start with him, he will give you all you need. Seek him
and he will help you walk in the way that is right. The more
time you spend with him, the more your character and
perspective will begin to reflect his.

How can you earnestly seek God's presence today?

He Knows Us

Just as a father has compassion on his children,
So the LORD has compassion on those who fear Him.
For He Himself knows our form;
He is mindful that we are nothing but dust.

PSALM 103:13-14 NASB

God isn't deluded about our capabilities. He knows us as his children, and he created us from dust at the beginning. He has so much compassion for us—more than we can imagine! His mercy never runs out, and his kindness isn't a limited resource. Every time we come to our Father, he is full of love for us, even though he knows each of our failures and limitations. He is mindful of us, and he has compassion when we turn to him.

You don't have to pretend to be something you are not. You don't have to hide your weaknesses or be ashamed of your mistakes. He welcomes you with open arms, and he knows you fully. His compassion is abundant for those who fear him. Turn to him and give him your life because he is worthy of your devotion.

How have you experienced God's compassion?

Complete Perfection

God surveyed all he had made and said, "I love it!"
For it pleased him greatly.

GENESIS 1:31 TPT

Have you ever made something and stepped back, admiring how lovely it was? This is what God did after he created the world. Before man was formed and woman created, God loved the world he made. He expertly wove every part of creation together, and he was happy with it. Every aspect of creation existed in that moment, fresh, untainted, and perfect.

The world around you may seem like a far cry from the original picture God painted. The earth is riddled with catastrophes that man's hands have made. Remember that one day everything will be made right. When Jesus returns, all of creation will once again be perfect. Everything that is lost will be found, and everything broken will be fixed. Instead of falling into despair, let the chaos of the world fill you with greater anticipation for the day it is made perfect again.

Spend some time imagining
what a perfect earth might look like.

Forgiveness

Be kind to one another, tenderhearted, forgiving one another, even as God in Christ forgave you.

EPHESIANS 4:32 NKJV

Scripture urges us to embrace a life of forgiveness. Even when it's painful, we are asked to offer forgiveness to those who hurt us. The good news is we don't need to muster up the strength to forgive. Our ability to do it comes from the abundant grace we've already been given. The more we realize how much God has forgiven us, the more readily we can do the same for others.

Forgiveness is often more transformational for you than the person you're offering it to. It's possible they might not even know you are overlooking their wrongs. For you, offering forgiveness softens your heart and allows mercy to reign in your life. It uproots bitterness that may have taken root, and it sets you free from judgement and criticism. God is not stingy with forgiveness, and you can reflect his character by offering it to others when they make mistakes.

Who do you need to forgive?

May

We are his workmanship,
created in Christ Jesus for good works,
which God prepared beforehand,
that we should walk in them.

Ephesians 2:10 ESV

Always New

The LORD's love never ends;
his mercies never stop.
They are new every morning;
LORD, your loyalty is great.

LAMENTATIONS 3:22-23 NCV

When we need encouragement, we can let Scripture wash over us and bring refreshment. We can invite the Lord into whatever situation we are facing and hold fast to what he says is true. His love never ends, and his mercies never stop. He is with us through each challenge, struggle, and sorrow we face. He is loyal to each of us, and there is nothing he cannot redeem. He is ours, and we are his.

If you need a new dose of his mercy, consider it done. If you need a fresh encounter with his love, open wide the gates of your heart and welcome the King of glory to come in. He knows exactly what you need, and he is always generous with his resources. When you put your hope in him, you will not be disappointed. Seek his presence and let him renew your spirit.

*Turn your heart toward God today
and embrace the mercy he bestows on you.*

Hopeful Waiting

The LORD is good to those who wait for him,
to the person who seeks him.
It is good to wait quietly
for salvation from the LORD.

LAMENTATIONS 3:25-26 CSB

When we wait on the Lord, we do not wait without hope.
We don't need to sit and wonder if he will come through.
He is good to those who wait for him. He is faithful to
those who seek him. Even when his timing doesn't line up
with our preferences, we can remain steady. Even when our
circumstances seem discouraging, we can remain hopeful.

Trust the Lord. His timing is perfect—never too early or
too late. He will bring the breakthrough you need at just the
right time. His Word is reliable, and he promises to be good
to you while you wait. He will never withhold his presence
from you, and he will ensure you are taken care of. Will you
learn to rest in the waiting?

Do you struggle to wait quietly?
Ask God to strengthen your resolve today.

Right on Time

The Lord isn't really being slow about his promise,
as some people think. No, he is being patient for your sake.
He does not want anyone to be destroyed,
but wants everyone to repent.

2 PETER 3:9 NLT

God's patience is intricately interwoven with mercy.
Though we long for Jesus to return and make all things new,
it is best to trust God's timing. On our worst days, when it's
hard to muster up any more perseverance, it's important to
remember that God's plan is perfect. He will come back and
usher in his kingdom at just the right time. He doesn't want
a single one of his children to be apart from him, so he will
wait until as many hearts as possible turn to him.

You are part of a much larger story than what you see
around you. God's plan for redemption encompasses all
that has ever been and all that is yet to come. When his
eternal kingdom is fully established it will include every
person who has ever turned their heart toward him. He will
not leave a single one of his children behind. As you wait,
remember that he knows exactly what he is doing.

*Today, consider God's great mercy as he waits
for each of his children to seek him.*

Flawless Wisdom

"Every word of God is flawless;
he is a shield to those who take refuge in him."

PROVERBS 30:5 NIV

Everything God says and does is flawless. We can trust his Word to guide us, and we can rely on his strength when we are weak. Even though our access to information is unprecedented, God should still be our highest standard. There is no level of academic or intellectual achievement that can surpass the wisdom of God. Don't let the clanging opinions that surround you overtake the steady and superior opinion of God.

While you look to the perfection of God remember that he showers you with grace. He is your refuge and your strength. He does not hold his perfection over your head or shame you for not being able to match it. He does not set impossible goals for you, and he is not bothered by your weaknesses. He joyfully and willingly offers to lift you up. He is delighted to hold you securely in his hands.

*Today, praise God for his perfection
and thank him for his grace.*

Good, Right, and True

*This light within you produces only
what is good and right and true.*

EPHESIANS 5:9 NLT

When Jesus ascended to heaven after his resurrection, he did not abandon us. He did not leave us alone to navigate life without him. He left his Spirit who leads, teaches, and encourages us. When the Spirit is within us, he will produce things in our lives that are good, right, and true. This is how we know he is at work. The light within us will never produce something that is contradictory to the perfect character of God.

As you follow Jesus and seek to embody his teachings, you'll notice the Spirit at work in your life. You'll recognize his leadership, and you'll become familiar with the way he guides you toward truth. The more you open your heart to him, the more you'll recognize his voice and trust his instructions.

*Ask God to show you his light in your life and practice
following the urging of the Spirit.*

Refreshing Waters

"Listen! Are you thirsty for more?
Come to the refreshing waters and drink.
Even if you have no money, come, buy, and eat.
Yes, come and buy all the wine and milk you
desire—it won't cost a thing."

ISAIAH 55:1 TPT

What an incredible invitation we find in today's verse. If we are thirsty for more of God, there is nothing holding us back. Our thirst can absolutely be quenched. We don't have to offer anything in exchange. God welcomes us to freely partake of all we need. The price has already been paid and nothing can disqualify or preclude us from experiencing the goodness of God's presence.

Through Christ, there is refreshing for your soul. In the fellowship of God, there is more than you can imagine ever needing. He is abundant and generous, and you will never have to beg for your daily bread. You are invited to be refreshed in the living waters of his presence. Don't despair when you can find satisfaction for your soul's deepest longings in the presence of your Maker.

Spend some time in the presence of the Lord,
turning your heart toward his goodness.

Walk with Him

"Stand by the ways and see and ask for the ancient paths,
Where the good way is, and walk in it;
Then you will find a resting place for your souls."

JEREMIAH 6:16 NASB

There are times we stray from the path we know is right. We make mistakes and allow our emotions or our weaknesses to guide us. No matter how far off track we wander, it is never too late to course correct. God is near, and he remains faithful no matter how much we deviate from where we should be. He never loses sight of us, and he is never discouraged by our shortcomings.

Though it may be difficult to grasp, God's ability to keep you steady is greater than your ability to faulter. Trust that he is capable of guiding you. As you follow him, he will give you peace in exchange for anxious striving. He will equip you to live rightly, and he will fill your soul with satisfaction that can only come from him. If your desire is to be near him, he will guide you and walk with you each step of the way.

When have you experienced the rest that comes
from walking in God's way?

Benefits of Both

Enthusiasm without knowledge is not good.
If you act too quickly, you might make a mistake.

PROVERBS 19:2 NCV

Enthusiasm can provide great motivation to start, but it is not always a good predictor of an outcome. Enthusiasm with knowledge, however, is an incredible force. Passion for what we are doing allows us to get off the sidelines and act while knowledge keeps our momentum steady and productive. Knowledge can keep us moving when newness has worn off and consistency and follow through are required.

It's easy to be passionate about a subject or task. Without passion you may never take risks or step out in faith. At the same time, embrace the steady wisdom of God. Ask him for guidance and be diligent in seeking knowledge. Passion without knowledge is foolish while knowledge without passion can feel dry or empty. Yield your actions and emotions to God and aim to have both passion and knowledge in your life.

Are you more prone to elevate passion or knowledge in your decision making?

Only Mercy

When God our Savior revealed his kindess and love, he
saved us, not because of the righteous things we had done,
but because of his mercy. He washed away our sins, giving
us a new birth and new life through the Holy Spirit.

TITUS 3:4-5 NLT

Our actions are not part of the equation when it comes
to salvation. God didn't come to save us because of
anything good we've done. His redemption is based on his
extravagant mercy, overpowering love, and extraordinary
compassion. We cannot take credit for any of it. We cannot
pat ourselves on the back or claim that we deserve the gifts
God has given us.

You don't have to do anything to earn the favor of God. You
don't have to prove yourself to him, and you don't have to
maintain your reputation with him. He sees you perfectly
and his opinion of you will never change. No matter what,
he sees you with mercy. Soften your heart and remember
that you are worthy of his love. You matter because he says
you do. There is nothing that qualifies or disqualifies you
from his goodness.

Today, let God wash away your sins and give you new life.

Trust and Do

Trust in the LORD and do what is good;
dwell in the land and live securely.

PSALM 37:3 CSB

The more we trust the Lord the more easily we will do what is good in our own lives. When we diligently seek his presence, we will learn to love with he loves, and our actions will reflect his character. As we experience his faithfulness, loyal love, and generous mercy we will in turn treat others the same way.

When you trust in the Lord you make room in your life for doing good. This is because your energy isn't being spent on anxiety, rumination, doubt, or pride. When you surrender to him, he takes care of you. You can live securely and focus on loving and serving others. You don't have to be bound up by your own problems because you know that God is in control.

What area of your life could use more trust?

Good Refuge

The LORD is good,
a refuge in times of trouble.
He cares for those who trust in him.

NAHUM 1:7 NIV

There will be times in life when the challenges seem to outweigh the joys. This does not mean that the power of God's presence has become less accessible. God is close to the brokenhearted, and he is near to those who are in trouble. He helps those who cry out to him, and he saves those who put their hope in him. In times of desperate reliance, we can experience the power of his goodness more poignantly than when we take it for granted.

If you need a place of refuge today, you can find it in God. He isn't far away, and he longs for you to lean on him. Put your trust in him and believe that he will care for you. He sees exactly what you are going through, and he knows precisely how it is impacting you. He can untangle your emotions and give you peace that surpasses understanding. If you are in trouble, run into the steady arms of your heavenly Father.

How has the Lord's presence been a comfort to you?

All Your Days

Surely your goodness and unfailing love
will pursue me all the days of my life,
and I will live in the house of the LORD forever.

PSALM 23:6 NLT

It is beautiful to be convinced of God's love. As we embrace it, his love becomes our confidence and our shield. It fills us with hope, even when our circumstances are not ideal. His love carries us through the trials of this life as we collectively long for the perfection of his kingdom. No matter how long we live, we can be sure that we will never be without God's presence. As we seek him, he fills our lives with goodness and surrounds us with his love.

Suffering and trials are inevitable. You know this to be true. Don't forget that God's goodness is also inevitable. As long as you live, there are opportunities to rejoice in what God has done for you. You will be discouraged and overwhelmed if you consistently focus on what is challenging. Remember that God promises to pursue you with goodness and love amid trials. You are never without his leadership, wisdom, or kindness.

How have you recently experienced God's goodness and love?

Greater Love

"Love your enemies, and do good, and lend, expecting
nothing in return, and your reward will be great, and
you will be sons of the Most High, for he is kind to the
ungrateful and the evil."

LUKE 6:35 ESV

It is not difficult to love those who already love us. If we
want to honor Scripture, we must extend our love toward
everyone. When we choose to operate according to God's
mercy, it doesn't stop with those who honor and respect
us. We are called to love extravagantly regardless of
circumstances. Loving our enemies requires sacrifice, but it
is good and right. We may never get anything in return, but
it is worth it.

Jesus calls you to love others beyond your own abilities. He
knows that on your own, you cannot love like he can. He
loves you sacrificially and extravagantly first. As you receive
his love, you are able to extend it to those around you. You
do not give from an empty cup but from an overflowing
one. Through Christ you can generously lay your life down
and expect nothing in return.

How can you grow in love today?

Notice the Forgotten

One who is gracious to a poor person lends to the LORD,
And He will repay him for his good deed.

PROVERBS 19:17 NASB

We are often told that if we budget well, work hard, and invest wisely, we will find success. While these are admirable and wise habits, they are not supposed to be on the top of our priority list. Budgeting is wonderful, but if the fruit it bears is selfishness, then we should rethink our plan. Working hard is important, but if we place work above relationships, we should adjust our behavior. Investing our finances wisely is smart, but if this becomes our source of security, we are going about it in the wrong way.

If you want to honor God with your resources, you cannot overlook the poor and needy. Scripture consistently affirms how God views people who the world typically forgets. Not only does he urge you to be generous toward them, but he promises to repay your good deeds. You can be confident that if God is the one repaying you, you will be more than adequately compensated. Godly generosity is rooted in the assurance that God has more than enough to take care of each of his children.

How can you grow in generosity toward the poor?

Way of Life

Beloved children, our love can't be an abstract theory
we only talk about, but a way of life demonstrated
through our loving deeds.

1 JOHN 3:18 TPT

If all we do is talk about love, we are fooling ourselves.
True love requires actions and sacrifice. There is no point
in discussing our opinions of love or arguing over proper
execution. Instead, God's love should dictate the way
we live and how we treat others. It's easy to say that we
love others, but it is difficult to inconveniently our even
painfully lay our lives down. We must live out our beliefs or
they don't mean anything.

Love is rarely convenient and completely comfortable. If
your objective is to love others well, you will often sacrifice
your time, energy, and resources to help others. You cannot
constantly prioritize yourself or your opinions and still love
others well. The good news is that God doesn't ask you to
love others and then leave you desperate for love yourself.
He joyfully pours his love over your life first and then asks
you to share it with those around you.

How can you actively love others today?

Unusual Kindness

The natives showed us unusual kindness;
for they kindled a fire and made us all welcome,
because of the rain that was falling and because of the cold.

ACTS 28:2 NKJV

In today's Scripture Paul is referencing the kindness of the people of Malta. They were a gracious people, and their generosity blessed Paul. Unusual kindness is a gift wherever it is found; it can expand our hearts and increase our gratitude. What if we endeavored to treat others with unusual, extraordinary kindness? The kind that sticks with the recipient far after the encounter.

It is no small thing to choose generosity and kindness. You honor God when you choose to share your resources, bless others, and take care of those around you. When you welcome someone into your home, no matter what it looks like, you demonstrate the welcoming hospitality that God has shown to everyone without bias. Kindness is just one way you can show a desperate world the all-encompassing love of God.

Be remarkably kind in a practical way today.

Language of Empathy

Be happy with those who are happy,
and be sad with those who are sad.

ROMANS 12:15 NCV

When we share in the emotional state of someone else, we step into their reality for a little while. We acknowledge that what they feel is important and valuable. The ability to empathize with others allows us to love like God loves. He doesn't ever shame or embarrass us when we bring our feelings to him. He doesn't call us silly or tell us to stop feeling a certain way. Instead, he embraces us and surrounds us with his love. We are meant to do the same with others.

It is equally good to sit with a friend in grief and to celebrate their victories. Both are necessary and right. In either situation, your presence means so much more than your opinion. It doesn't matter if you think someone shouldn't be grieving a particular loss, grieve with them. Likewise, if someone is joyful, don't try to talk them down. When you meet someone where they're at, it shows that you care. When you share in someone's joys and sorrows, it shows you are capable of loving them regardless of their circumstances.

If someone shares something with you today,
meet them in their emotions.

Worthwhile Pursuit

In everything we do, we show that we are true ministers of God. We patiently endure troubles and hardships and calamities of every kind.

2 CORINTHIANS 6:4 NLT

The fruit of our lives reveals where our roots are planted. If we are rooted in the love of Christ, our lives will show it. In 2 Corinthians Paul lists some of the ways in which we reveal that we are God's ministers. Sincere love, purity, wisdom, patience, kindness, and endurance all show that he is at work in our lives.

When you invest your time, energy, and resources into growing your character, you will not be disappointed. The pursuit of godly character will add value to every area of your life. It will benefit your relationships, thought life, and work ethic. As you seek to live in a way that honors God, you will begin to notice an abundance of fruit.

Ask the Holy Spirit to highlight an area of your character in which you can pursue growth.

Keep Going

Let's not get tired of doing what is good. At just the right time we will reap a harvest of blessing if we don't give up.

GALATIANS 6:9 NLT

Paul's admonition in Galatians would be meaningless if he didn't recognize the human tendency to get tired. He wouldn't have warned us against getting tired of doing good if he didn't think it was a possibility. Our weariness is human and completely normal. This is why we need the encouragement of Scripture. We need to be reminded that a reward is coming if we persevere.

If you don't quit, you win. God will not turn you away at the finish line. Your life is not a timed race with impossible standards. Just keep going. In God's perfect timing, you will reap a harvest of blessing. While you may be struggling right now, don't quit. He is on your side, and he is taking every labored step right alongside you. Keep your eyes steadily on eternity with Christ and resolve to keep moving forward on the path God has set before you.

When you are tempted to give up, remember that God is with you through your trials.

Gentle Answers

A gentle answer turns away wrath,
but a harsh word stirs up anger.

PROVERBS 15:1 NIV

There is no weakness in being gentle. It takes tremendous
self-control and awareness to respond to a harsh word with
gentleness. Our natural reaction is to bite back and make
sure our opinion is known. We don't typically want to offer
gracious understanding. When we give in to our flesh and
use our words as weapons, we only add fuel to the fire.

It is wise to practice using gentle words. When emotions
are high, it's important to be quick to listen and slow to
speak. This gives you time to choose your words carefully,
to consider the other person's perspective, and to pursue
peace. A gentle answer does not mean that you need to
avoid the truth. Rather, it means that you speak with
kindness and intentionality.

How can you practice gentleness in the way you speak today?

Your Choice

Let not steadfast love and faithfulness forsake you;
bind them around your neck;
write them on the tablet of your heart.

PROVERBS 3:3 ESV

Scripture is full of recommendations for favor and success. Solomon reminds us that if we desire those things, we will carry steadfast love and faithfulness with us wherever we go. This means that every decision we make is based on those principles. Everything we say and do should be marked by love and faithfulness.

When you build your life around godly principles, you will not be disappointed. When you honor God's Word, his blessings will follow. You get to choose what is bound around your neck and written on the tablet of your heart. You can carry around negativity and cynicism, or you can deliberately be defined by steadfast love and faithfulness.

Which values have guided your decision making lately?

Friends not Slaves

> "No longer do I call you slaves, for the slave does not know what his master is doing; but I have called you friends, because all things that I have heard from My Father I have made known to you."

JOHN 15:15 NASB

Jesus did not come to the earth to reprimand us or to use our weaknesses against us. He did not come to hold his perfection over our heads or to point out everything we are doing wrong. Rather, he came as a friend to show us the way to the Father. His love sets us free and ushers us into God's eternal kingdom.

Jesus calls you his friend. Think about your closest friends and what your relationships with them look like. You likely share each other's sorrows and victories. You probably provide practical help to each other and are blessed by each other's company. The bottom line is that you have a relationship because you want one and you enjoy it. This is how Jesus wants to relate to you. He doesn't want you to be bound to him in obligation. He enjoys you, and he wants a relationship with you.

How can you cultivate a deeper friendship with Christ today?

He Redeems

"Do not fear, for I, your Kinsman-Redeemer, will rescue you.
I have called you by name, and you are mine."

ISAIAH 43:1 TPT

Fear is not a sign of failure. The fact that we feel afraid does not mean that we aren't strong enough. Rather, it is an opportunity to lean into the faithfulness of God. When something seems scary or downright impossible, we can allow our faith to strengthened by God's presence. He is undaunted, and we can claim his steadiness as our own.

God will not let you down. You can be courageous because he is dependable and faithful. He promises that he will rescue you, and you can take him at his word. He has always kept his promises, and he won't fail now. No matter what you are facing, God can redeem what is lost and fix what is broken. Your hope doesn't lie in your own fickle emotions but in his steadfast, unshakeable love.

When fear creeps in, let God strengthen you.

Fresh Clothes

Put on the new man which was created according to God,
in true righteousness and holiness.

EPHESIANS 4:24 NKJV

Without the grace of God, we may look at our lives and be dismayed by our shortcomings. It would be overwhelming to come face to face with our failures and have no way of fixing them. God in his great mercy, provides the answers to everything we need. He offers us complete transformation, not because we aren't good enough but because he is perfect and wants us to experience the abundant life he intended.

When you surrender your life to Jesus, you are made new. You can set aside your old ways of living and rejoice in your salvation. Instead of being bound to your failures, you can claim Christ's righteousness as your own. You are perfect because he is perfect. When you feel discouraged, remember that redemption and newness are always available to you in Christ.

Today, put on God's grace and love
and leave your shame behind.

Tell Him

People, trust God all the time.
Tell him all your problems,
because God is our protection.

PSALM 62:8 NCV

We can tell God anything, and he will not hold it against us. We don't have to organize our thoughts or make sure that we communicate clearly. We can share every fickle thought that flits across our mind, and he will know exactly what to do with it. When we consistently share our lives with him, we open ourselves up to being transformed by his wisdom and grace.

You can trust God all the time, no matter what. Don't hold anything back from him. Whatever you are struggling with today, take it to God. Bring him your fears, hurt, and even your embarrassing questions. He is not intimidated or bothered by any of it. Keep your heart soft toward him, and he will protect you. You can trust him with every part of your life.

What problems do you tend to keep to yourself?

Only Grace

By the grace of God I am what I am, and his grace toward me was in vain. On the contrary, I worked harder than any of them, yet not I, but the grace of God that was with me.

1 Corinthians 15:10 CSB

It is not necessary to work for our place in God's family. A child should not earn the love of their parents, and we don't earn the affection of our heavenly Father. Even if we put all of our effort into being good enough, it would all be in vain. God's love for us existed before we were even born. We cannot add to its vastness or steal from its perfection. His love exists outside of our ability to earn or alter it. Grace is our only means of experiencing God's love.

Your greatest successes cannot earn you God's love, and your greatest failures cannot deem you ineligible. His grace is what allows you to experience his love. You are saved because of the undeserved favor that he pours upon your life. No matter how hard you work, you will never achieve a more secure salvation than what Christ has established for you. His work on the cross is what enables you to be transformed and redeemed.

Where do you see unnecessary striving in your life?

Full of Hope

Worship Christ as Lord of your life. And if someone asks about your hope as a believer, always be ready to explain it.

1 Peter 3:15 NLT

As believers, our lives are defined by hope. Our greatest hope is that one day Jesus will come back and restore all things. Everything will be made new, and we will spend eternity in the perfect presence of God. There is nothing we can experience on earth that can take this hope away from us. No matter how bad things get, we know that perfection is coming.

You are meant to share the hope you've been given. The world is desperate for it. Imagine thinking the trials of this life lead to nothing. Without a promised destination, any journey is difficult to navigate. If you are asked, be ready to explain the reason for your perseverance and strength. You can endure many trials because of what Jesus has done for you and all he promises to do in the future.

How can you be ready to share your hope?

Without Words

The Spirit helps us in our weakness. We do not know what we ought to pray for, but the Spirit himself intercedes for us through wordless groans.

ROMANS 8:26 NIV

The Holy Spirit is our great helper. He is our teacher, counselor, and friend. We are never alone because he is always with us. If we want to faithfully follow Jesus for all our days, we need the help of the Spirit. We cannot do it alone. There are times when our weaknesses are overwhelming, and we desperately need someone to take our hand and lead us. When our own limitations seem monumental, the Holy Spirit helps us put one foot in front of the other.

When you have the Holy Spirit, you are never at a loss. Whether you can perfectly articulate your needs, or you are overwhelmed by your emotions, the Holy Spirit is your advocate. He intercedes for you. He can take your jumbled heart and decipher it perfectly. He knows exactly what you need and why you feel the way you do. When you are led by the Spirit, he will help you with your weaknesses.

How can you daily depend on the Spirit?

Fresh Revelation

All Scripture is breathed out by God and profitable for teaching, for reproof, for correction, and for training in righteousness, that the man of God may be complete, equipped for every good work.

2 TIMOTHY 3:16-17 ESV

The Word of God is filled with teachings, wisdom, and principles to strengthen us. The book of Proverbs has practical wisdom for how to live. The epistles highlight real-life struggles and help us to reach beyond them to the hope of Christ. The gospels reveal who Jesus was, who he is, and the promise of who he will continue to be.

When was the last time you felt encouraged, challenged, or inspired by Scripture? The Holy Spirit loves to reveal the heart of God through the Word. He will help you move beyond your own understanding and embrace God's perspective. Soften your heart and ask him to give you fresh revelation as you read Scripture and seek to apply it to your life.

Invite the Holy Spirit to give you
a deeper understanding of the Word.

Guideposts

"Set up roadmarks for yourself,
Place guideposts for yourself;
Direct your mind to the highway,
The way by which you went."

JEREMIAH 31:21 NASB

When the Israelites wandered in the desert, God had them put remembrance stones in places where he moved on their behalf. He performed miracles for them, and he knew they would be likely to forget. When difficult circumstances arose, the Israelites were quick to blame God and lose sight of how he had sustained them the whole time they wandered. God wanted to them set up guideposts so they might be reminded of his faithfulness.

You can do the same in your personal walk with God. The ritual of remembering what God has done will give you hope and will strengthen your faith. Dwell on your history with God and take note of all he's done for you. When you encounter trials, you'll have a deep well of memories to draw from. You'll be able to confidently declare that God has been faithful to you, and he will continue to be faithful for all your days.

*Write down as many instances of God's help
as you can remember.*

Wonderful Treasures

Lord, how wonderful you are!
You have stored up so many good things for us,
like a treasure chest heaped up
and spilling over with blessings—
all for those who honor and worship you!

PSALM 31:19 TPT

There are innumerable blessings stored up for those who honor the Lord and choose to worship him. As we offer him our lives, he proves himself faithful over and over again. He leads us through the joys and sorrows of this life, and he promises that perfection is waiting for us in eternity. We offer him our devotion and he does not leave us empty handed.

It is always worth it to follow the Lord. Though you will experience suffering on earth, be assured that treasures are being stored up for you in heaven. A day will come when you reap the rewards of your worship and obedience. Don't be dismayed when you don't experience those treasures on earth. God will keep his word. He does not make promises he cannot keep.

What treasures have you already found from honoring God?

June

In Christ we were chosen to be
God's people, because from the very
beginning God had decided this
in keeping with his plan.

EPHESIANS 1:11 NCV

Choose Compassion

Be of one mind, having compassion for one another.

1 Peter 3:8 NKJV

God asks each of us to be compassionate and tenderhearted. These qualities don't always line up with how we feel. In some situations, it will take a deliberate decision to embrace the selfless love of Christ. We are often tempted to put our needs first, but this is not how we have been called to live. Even when others reject or hate us, we don't choose the same attitude toward them. We can choose the higher road and lovingly rise above.

This may sound too lofty to live out, but you can practice it in little ways. Steadily, you will build your strength, and it will become easier. Remember God is with you every step of the way. He equips you to love others as he does, and he rewards you when you do the right thing. Scripture promises that you will inherit a blessing when you bless others.

How can you practice having compassion
for those around you today?

Approach Confidently

Let us, then, feel very sure that we can come before God's throne where there is grace. There we can receive mercy and grace to help us when we need it.

HEBREWS 4:16 NCV

There is so much mercy in the presence of God. There is grace to help us whenever we need it. This is what God's Word promises, and there is no reason to keep ourselves way from his throne. No matter how far we feel from him in the moment, we must remember that there is nothing holding us back from him. Let us approach his gracious presence with the expectation that he is willing and able to help us.

Let today's Scripture encourage if you and give you confidence in how God sees you. He has given you an open invitation to his throne. He doesn't say things out of politeness or obligation; he doesn't make promises he can't keep. If he says you are welcome to receive mercy and grace in his presence, then it is true and reliable. No matter what you are facing today, you can take it God and lay it at his feet.

Go to the Lord, just as you are today.

Builders

Each one of us is to please his neighbor for his good,
to build him up.

ROMANS 15:2 CSB

Though we all have different jobs and roles, we are each
called to be good neighbors. This instruction is universal,
and it applies to everyone across the board. Building
each other up with wisdom, compassion, and authentic
connection is a privilege. When we seek to serve one
another in love, our hearts remain soft and we are able to
learn, pivot, and repair when necessary.

It is wonderful to pour into someone else's life, and it is
a blessing to receive encouragement when you need it.
You were created for this type of connection—both the
giving and receiving of it. There is never a shortage of
opportunities to lift up the people in your life. Your words,
the way you listen, and the way you respond to needs can
either build up or tear down. Choose to be the kind of
person who thoughtfully considers the needs and emotions
of each person you come across.

How can you build up your neighbor today?

Open Your Ears

"Come to me with your ears wide open.
Listen, and you will find life.
I will make an everlasting covenant with you.
I will give you all the unfailing love I promised to David."

ISAIAH 55:3 NLT

There is a wealth of life-giving wisdom in the presence of God. Whenever we go to him, listening for his voice and opening our hearts to his Spirit, we receive just what we need. When we seek him, he faithfully responds. When we ask him for help, we trust that he won't leave us hanging.

Though you may not know the fullness of God's thoughts, he always has something to share with you. As you make room for him, tuning your ears to his voice, you will find more than enough peace, hope, and love to satisfy your needs. Through Christ, he has made a covenant with you, and he will uphold every part of it. He loves to open his hands and satisfy the needs of his children.

Listen for God's voice and you will find life.

Whatever You Do

Whatever you do, work at it with all your heart, as working for the Lord, not for human masters, since you know that you will receive an inheritance from the Lord as a reward.

COLOSSIANS 3:23-24 NIV

We all have the freedom to try different things and to choose where we direct our attention, skills, and resources. The important thing isn't exactly what we do but that we do it wholeheartedly for the Lord. He is far less concerned with the details than we might realize. It's more important to live according to Godly principles than to fret over the perfect execution of his will. He cares more about our hearts than the schedule of our days.

Is your work wholeheartedly committed to the Lord? Or are you more concerned with your personal goals and how you might appear? There is no shame in stumbling in this area. It's easy to get wrapped up in the concerns of the world, constantly worried about the opinions and expectations of others. Remember that no status, success, or lack thereof matters more than God's standard. Work unto him and let him pour his mercy and grace over your life.

Today, commit your tasks to the Lord
and seek to honor him above all else.

More than Able

"Nothing will be impossible with God."

LUKE 1:37 ESV

Today's verse comes from Gabriel's conversation with Mary. He had just told her she would be the mother of the Messiah and her elderly aunt, Elizabeth, would also give birth to a son. What seemed completely impossible was not when God intervened. Thousands of years prior God had promised he would one day redeem his people. He was faithful even when it seemed like hope was lost.

God does not make promises he cannot keep. He is more than able to accomplish everything he says. He is creative, powerful, and loyal to his word. He might not move according to your timeline, but that doesn't mean he isn't faithful. His ways are higher than yours, and you can trust he will do what is best. Even when progress doesn't look the way you want, keep trusting God for the impossible.

Give your hopeless, messy, and impossible situations to the Lord today.

Powerful Spirit

God has not given us a spirit of timidity,
but of power and love and discipline.

2 TIMOTHY 1:7 NASB

When we feel timid or insecure, it's important to remember
we have the Holy Spirit within us. He strengthens us when
we are weak, and he helps us live in a way that honors the
Lord. When we follow him, he equips us to live with power,
love, and discipline. These are the types of blessings God
promises to those who follow him. We often expect to see
material riches or smooth circumstances. Instead, following
God means we are transformed from the inside out.

Fulfilling your purpose for God is more about inner work
than what you might accomplish. Confidence is a gift
from God. Living with a sense of security and fortitude
is better than any physical gift you could receive. In any
circumstance, you can feel strong and unshakeable because
of who God is. Can you imagine how your life might be
different if you embodied power, love, and discipline in
every situation? God's Spirit within you empowers you to
do this.

Today, ask God to strengthen you from the inside out.

True Source

Out of him, the sustainer of everything, came everything,
and now everything finds fulfillment in him.
May all praise and honor be given to him forever! Amen!

ROMANS 11:36 TPT

In God, everything moves, breathes, and has its being. As the maker of everything, he is the only one who can sustain and fulfill every longing heart. He is the author of love and the giver of every good and perfect gift. He is the one who meets our weakness with his strength and satisfies the desires of our hearts. True fulfillment can only be found in him.

God knows what you need. He is aware of your physical requirements, and he knows what you are lacking internally. He can see all of you clearly and without obstruction. Furthermore, he is capable of prioritizing your needs. When you put your life in his hands, trust him to sustain you. While you might be convinced of how things should unfold, God is the only one who knows each detail of your days.

Glorify God as the source of all things
and trust him to sustain you as you follow him.

Even Then

Though I walk through the valley of the shadow of death,
I will fear no evil;
For You are with me.

PSALM 23:4 NKJV

God is with us through every valley and desert. There is never a time when we are alone or without the protection of his presence. We can walk confidently through whatever life sends our way because God is always with us. He is a good shepherd who faithfully takes care of his sheep no matter what. The threat of death and the darkest evil cannot overcome those who put their trust in him.

God knows every trial you will face. He isn't surprised by the suffering in your life. The presence of heartache does not mean you are far from God. In fact, the opposite is true. He promises to be with you even when you are lost in despair or desperation. He will never leave you. His presence is your strength, and you can lean on him to guide you through whatever you are facing.

God's purpose for you does not pause
when you are in a valley. Trust him even then.

No Holding Back

The LORD God is like a sun and shield;
the LORD gives us kindness and honor.
He does not hold back anything good
from those whose lives are innocent.

PSALM 84:11 NCV

When we take our sin and weakness into account, how can
we possibly be innocent? We fail on a daily basis, and we
certainly cannot be considered without fault. This is why
we must desperately cling to Christ's work on the cross.
Through the cross, his righteousness becomes our own.
Through his sacrifice, we are made pure and clean. We are
innocent only because of what he has done for us.

As you cling to the righteousness of Christ, God will
not hold back anything good from you. You have been
welcomed into his kingdom, and you have access to the vast
resources found there. When you are in need, remember
God desires to give you good gifts. Run to him and lay your
cares at his feet. He is for you, not against you. He sustains
and protects those who follow him.

Do you believe God wants to give you good gifts?
Why or why not?

Present Help

> "The LORD is the one who will go before you.
> He will be with you; he will not leave you or abandon you.
> Do not be afraid or discouraged."
>
> DEUTERONOMY 31:8 CSB

Wherever we are, God is with us. Whatever we are facing, God is not surprised by it. He goes before us into every challenge and circumstance. Not only is he present but he equips us to navigate each season of our lives. We may never know the lengths he has gone to prepare us for the challenges we face. He perfectly weaves the details of the universe together, and he faithfully sees us through each of our days. There is no limit to his knowledge, and there is nothing he cannot do for us.

Take a deep breath and let the presence of God comfort you. Even when you don't feel like it, he is with you. Even when you are convinced he has abandoned you, the truth says otherwise. When you feel alone, declare his promises over your life. Remind yourself of his faithfulness and command your soul to trust in him. Faith is a muscle that can be strengthened. The more you flex it, the more quickly you will be assured of his presence in times of trouble.

*Memorize today's verse and recite it when despair
threatens to overcome you.*

Plenty of Room

"There is more than enough room in my Father's home.
If this were not so, would I have told you
that I am going to prepare a place for you?"

JOHN 14:2 NLT

What an incredible relief it is to know that God isn't limited in his love. His kingdom does not have a maximum capacity. He will never turn anyone away. There is no shortage of space in his heart or at his table. There is more than enough to satisfy the hunger of every soul. We can look toward our heavenly home with great anticipation and confidence.

When you are convinced of your place in God's heart and kingdom, you will live with a sense of peace and assurance. Without the pressure of striving for a position, you'll find yourself able to serve him with joy and a quiet spirit. When your hope comes from Jesus and his promise to provide you with an eternal home, the troubles of this life will diminish. This is not to say you won't experience hardship, but you won't be crushed or dismayed by its existence.

How can the hope of what's to come
impact the purpose of your days?

Learn from Mistakes

These things happened to them as examples and were written down as warnings for us, on whom the culmination of the ages has come.

1 CORINTHIANS 10:11 NIV

This Scripture refers to the disobedience of the Israelites. They experienced miracles firsthand and still did not trust God. Even though they saw his mighty works with their own eyes, they set their hearts upon evil. Those who did not follow him did not experience the blessings he had promised. They refused to turn toward him and accept the grace he was offering.

It is good to learn from the mistakes of others. No matter how often you make good choices, you are not perfect. Stay humble and soft hearted lest you think you don't need God. Look at the examples in Scripture and take those warnings seriously. Each day you have a choice to follow God with purpose or to go your own way. Today, choose the life and peace God so graciously offers you. His ways are so much better than your own.

What have you learned from your past mistakes?

Support

You will show me the way of life,
granting me the joy of your presence
and the pleasures of living with you forever.

PSALM 16:11 NLT

When we willingly place our lives in God's hands, we can be confident he will keep us steady. He faithfully leads each of us toward eternal life. He walks with us through our darkest days, most complicated trials, and most joyous victories. As we seek him, he blesses us with his presence and shows us the path of life.

Steady your heart and rejoice in God's unending faithfulness. If you have submitted your life to him, he will guide you every step of the way. He promises to lead you and show you the way. He is not aloof or uninterested in the details of your life. He wants to walk with you. He wants to have uninterrupted communion with you. You are his child, and it is his delight to lead you through each of your days.

*If you are struggling with which direction to go,
remember God has promised to show you the way.*

Don't Miss Out

Make sure that your character is free from the love of money,
being content with what you have; for He Himself has said,
"I will never desert you, nor will I ever abandon you."

Contentment does not happen by accident. We cannot
wait for our circumstances to be perfect before we practice
the discipline of contentment. There must be a deliberate
choice to accept what we have with thanksgiving. As
we acknowledge God's steadfast presence, we will gain
confidence that everything will be okay. Fretting about the
future and constantly striving for more material wealth will
not satisfy our souls.

If you are driven by the love of money, you will never be
satisfied. The pursuit of wealth is never ending. If you gauge
your satisfaction by the measure of what you have, you will
never be fulfilled. If you are constantly striving for more,
you'll miss God's gifts for the season you are currently in.
Contentment is the acknowledgement that you are grateful
for what you have while trusting God for what you lack.

*Surrender your worries to God
and be present in the season you are in.*

Endless Opportunity

Take advantage of every opportunity to be a blessing to others, especially to our brothers and sisters in the family of faith!

GALATIANS 6:10 TPT

It is a privilege to partner with God in blessing others. Caring for others builds them up, but it also increases our capacity for kindness, compassion, and joy. While it is a blessing to enrich the lives of those around us, sometimes it is painful, inconvenient, and complicated. In those times, we must rely on the truth of Scripture. We have been clearly asked to take every opportunity to help whoever we can.

Even when it's not easy, you can be sure that blessing others is the will of God. If you ever struggle to understand your purpose, you can start by loving others. You will not go wrong when your main goal is to encourage, serve, and lift up those around you. Whether you reap the rewards in this life or the next, your good deeds are seen. God will faithfully take care of you as you take care of others.

Take every opportunity to be intentionally encouraging to others today.

New Habits

Let no corrupt word proceed out of your mouth,
but what is good for necessary edification,
that it may impart grace to the hearers.

EPHESIANS 4:29 NKJV

We are not expected to be perfect, but we should take ownership of our speech. The words we say are important. Our speech has the power to lift others up or tear them down. We each have a personal responsibility to be aware of what we say and how we say it. We should carefully consider everything that comes out of our mouths and make sure that our words align with the character of God.

Especially if you've formed a habit of negativity, it can be difficult to tame your tongue. Perhaps you easily fall into the trap of gossip or complaint. The unfortunate truth is those habits not only hurt others, but they cause bitterness and discontent to grow in your own heart. Neither of those things are God's best for you. Invite the Holy Spirit to soften your heart and help you build new practices.

Evaluate whether you need to change the way you talk to or about others.

Power to Accomplish

We keep on praying for you, asking our God to enable you
to live a life worthy of his call. May he give you the power to
accomplish all the good things your faith prompts you to do.

1 Thessalonians 1:11 nlt

God has called each of us to live in a way that is foreign to
our flesh. He knows we are prone to wander, and he knows
we can be fickle minded. He's very aware of our weaknesses,
yet he calls us anyway. He urges us to live a life of faith, and
he equips us to do it. As we reach out to him, he empowers
us to follow his ways. He faithfully gives us what we need,
and he encourages us along the way.

If your purpose is rooted in honoring God, he will surely
help you accomplish it. If your goal is to faithfully follow
him, he will give you the power to do it. Even when
situations seem impossible, or your weakness stands in the
way, he will not abandon you. When you are prompted by
faith to do something, trust him to equip you. He knows
exactly what you need, and he is abundantly generous.

*Trust God to enable you instead of being disheartened
by goals that seem impossible.*

No Fear

The LORD is my light and my salvation—
whom should I fear?

PSALM 27:1 CSB

There are plenty of opportunities in life to be afraid. If we let anxiety rule our emotions, it will swiftly take over. It will creep into every situation if we let it, demanding our energy and stealing our peace. Instead of letting fear dictate the decisions we make, we can rely on the unlimited strength of the Lord. He is able to carry us through every situation we face. If we stay anchored to him, we will remain steady no matter what we are threatened with.

Yielding your life to the leadership of the Lord doesn't guarantee an easy path. However, it does give you full access to overarching peace, clarifying wisdom, and the comfort of his presence. When fear threatens to overtake you, run to the safety of his arms. Tell him your deepest fears and most frustrating anxieties. Let him calm your mind and give you peace.

What fear have you been holding on to?

Continual Search

Search for the LORD and for his strength;
continually seek him.

1 CHRONICLES 16:11 NLT

Communion with God is not a one-time occurrence. We aren't supposed to grasp ahold of salvation and then stop looking for him. We are meant to seek him for all our days. We will inevitably wander toward the direction of our gaze, and we typically find what we are looking for. This is why we must direct our focus and worship on the Creator. He is meant to be the object of our affection.

The presence of God is what your soul longs for. No matter what you are lacking, he is the one who has what you need. Let your life be defined by the continuous pursuit of his love. There is no greater treasure in heaven or earth. Don't give up your search for him. Seek to follow him in all you do, and you won't be disappointed. Through every high and every low, you will see that he is worth the pursuit.

How can you actively seek the Lord today?

Inspired and Encouraged

When I called, you answered me;
you greatly emboldened me.

PSALM 138:3 NIV

God is ready to help in times of trouble. He answers us when we call, and he strengthens us from the inside out. Our circumstances may not change, but the way we deal with them can be shifted to line up with God's character and perspective. He equips us to navigate our days. Our problems shift drastically when we have the right tools to manage them. By his grace, we cry out to him, and he offers us the strength we need.

Sometimes your prayers won't be answered the way you hoped. God's promises often won't follow your timeline or preferences. Even when the details don't look how you want, his presence is always near. You can be confident that he will not ignore you when you call out to him. When you need strength, run to God first. He is the only one who can truly embolden you to face whatever is looming before you.

*Don't try to muster up strength
when it's supposed to come from God.*

No Shame

"Fear not, for you will not be ashamed;
be not confounded, for you will not be disgraced;
for you will forget the shame of your youth,
and the reproach of your widowhood
you will remember no more."

ISAIAH 54:4 ESV

God does not promote shame. He doesn't expect us to wallow in our mistakes. When we miss the mark, he meets us with mercy. When we pour our hearts out to him, he offers the comfort of his embrace. When we kneel in surrender at the cross, he cleanses us of all iniquity. His forgiveness is final and complete.

You are not expected to make perfect choices every moment of your life. You are human, and you will surely stumble or even fall from time to time. What matters most is your ability to humbly confess your sin and trust in God's unending mercy. If he says his forgiveness is complete, it is. If he wipes the slate clean, you don't have to question it. Carrying around shame and regret will not lead to anything but a life that is stifled and stuck in the past.

*Confess your sins, repent, and lean wholeheartedly
on the power of God's forgiveness.*

Be Courageous

"Be strong, and let's show ourselves courageous for the
benefit of our people and the cities of our God;
and may the LORD do what is good in His sight."

1 CHRONICLES 19:13 NASB

We cannot control God. We can't dictate what he should
do or how he should do it. He is the author of all that is
good, perfect, and true. His nature never changes, and
we can put our trust in him. We don't have to strive for
control or understand the nuances of how he moves. As we
trust him to do what is right, we grow in confidence of his
faithfulness.

God is in control of your life. Be strong and courageous and
trust him to work out the details. Surrender control to him
and let him take his rightful place on the throne of your
life. Your faithful trust in him, despite trials and suffering,
is a testimony to the people around you. It benefits the
body when you choose to boldly lean on God's promises.
It encourages others to also find their strength in the
unending goodness of God.

*Think of a time when you've been inspired
by the courage of others.*

Step Out

"Come and join me," Jesus replied.
So Peter stepped out onto the water
and began to walk toward Jesus.

MATTHEW 14:29 TPT

Jesus invited Peter to step out of the boat into an impossible situation. Peter boldly walked toward him and only began to sink when doubt flooded his mind. Whether he took one step or walked a mile upon the waves, a miracle happened! He did something that no one else would ever do. Even when Peter sank, Jesus immediately reached out his hand. He didn't hesitate or scold Peter before he saved him.

There will be times in your life when God asks you to step out in faith. No matter how many steps you take, he is by your side. He doesn't ask you to do the impossible and then leave you to flounder when you are in over your head. His hand is steady, and he is always with you. Keep your eyes fixed on Jesus and answer his call to step out of the boat. Join him in faith and rely on his strength.

Take a step of faith, and trust God's love to keep you steady.

Overarching Purpose

Having been justified by faith, we have peace with God through our Lord Jesus Christ, through whom also we have access by faith into this grace in which we stand, and rejoice in hope of the glory of God.

ROMANS 5:1-2 NKJV

As believers, we are justified by faith. Justification means we can stand blamelessly before God. Our sin cannot coexist with God's perfection. Jesus' sacrifice and resurrection set us free from the power of sin and death. When we put our faith in him, we are seen by God as though we are without fault. None of this is possible without faith. We must boldly believe that Christ's work on the cross is enough.

It's so easy to get wrapped up in the meaning of life. Don't fret over fulfilling your purpose or being faithful to God's calling in your life. His purposes for you are not complicated or unattainable. Remember you have been given great freedom through Jesus. Seek to share this freedom with everyone you can, and you won't go astray. Be extravagantly generous with the hope you have received.

How can you practically share the freedom and hope you have found?

Faith-filled Actions

People are made right with God by what they do,
not by faith only.

JAMES 2:24 NCV

Without faith, we cannot love God. We cannot see him face to face, so we must step outside what is tangible and embrace the intangible. Faith is paramount, but our actions matter just as much. We must live out what we believe. The grace we've been given must transform the way we live. It's important to address the discrepancies in our faith. Our actions should reflect the truth we claim to believe.

Your actions reveal your underlying belief systems. The way you treat people and how you spend your time shows what your priorities are. The way you live should be an overflow of what Christ has done for you. You can't claim to follow Jesus but refuse to live in a way that reflects his character. Keep your heart soft by delighting in the Word and being open to the leadership of the Holy Spirit. He will faithfully transform your heart day by day.

How do your actions match what you say you believe?

Practical Service

> "I was hungry and you gave me something to eat;
> I was thirsty and you gave me something to drink;
> I was a stranger and you took me in; I was naked and you
> clothed me; I was sick and you took care of me;
> I was in prison and you visited me."

MATTHEW 25:35-36 CSB

Sharing God's love can be as simple as noticing a need and meeting it with the resources we have. No matter how humble it may be, we can each share a meal or offer someone a drink. Our willingness to be generous reflects Christ's willingness to sacrifice his very life for us.

Sometimes, hospitality comes with a price. Sharing your resources with those in need might mean that you experience some discomfort or inconvenience. When this happens, remember that Jesus has made a far greater sacrifice for you. He laid his life down with humility and willingness, without disparaging humanity for being needy. Partner with him and do your best to share with those who are overlooked or forgotten.

How can you sacrifice your comfort for someone else today?

Safe Paths

People with integrity walk safely,
but those who follow crooked paths will be exposed.

PROVERBS 10:9 NLT

When we walk with integrity, we tread the safest path possible. This is because we have nothing to hide or cover up. We don't have to walk in fear, wondering if someone will uncover our failures. Practicing truthfulness protects us from the threat of exposure. Integrity gives us peace of mind, safety, and confidence that our actions are God-honoring.

Having integrity is not something that happens by accident. It is a quality that requires practice and intentionality. Pay attention to the little corners you cut. Notice how you might stretch the truth just a little bit. As you allow little habits of dishonesty into your life, you open the door to a larger integrity issue. Ask the Holy Spirit and he will help you develop a strong character. If your desire is to grow in integrity, he will accomplish it in your life.

*How have you experienced the safety
that comes from integrity?*

Small and Significant

"Whoever can be trusted with very little can also be trusted with much, and whoever is dishonest with very little will also be dishonest with much."

LUKE 16:10 NIV

Think of the children you have known in your lifetime. If their parents used common sense, they didn't give those children greater responsibilities than they could handle. No one asks a two-year-old to do the dishes and expects them to be spotless. It doesn't make sense to ask a nine-year-old to drive to the grocery store and pick up milk. Children must steadily grow in the area of responsibility and freedom.

The same is true in your own life. If you want to be trusted with something of significance, you must prove that you are capable. Conversely, if your actions prove you are irresponsible, you won't be given heavy responsibilities. If you want to grow in responsibility, you must first grow in trustworthiness and reliability.

Focus on today's responsibilities and handle them well.

Still Working

He who began a good work in you will bring it to
completion at the day of Jesus Christ.

PHILIPPIANS 1:6 ESV

We cannot possibly see the full picture of our lives. As such,
we easily get tangled in the day-to-day details. We base
our failures and success on our perceptions, and we hold
ourselves to timelines that we've decided are reasonable.
Instead, we should remember that God is the one truly in
control. He is the one who sovereignly sees every detail of our
lives. His perception is perfect, and he will faithfully carry out
his purposes for each person who calls upon his name.

You are not finished. Don't despair over the parts of your
life that don't look how you want. Surrender to the Lord
and trust his timing over your own. He will lead you in the
right way. He won't let a minute of your life go to waste.
He is capable of using each of your experiences, positive or
negative, to accomplish his purposes in your life. Relax and
remember he has your story under control.

Even when you can't see it, God is still working in your life.

July

In Christ we were chosen to be God's people, because from the very beginning God had decided this in keeping with his plan.

EPHESIANS 1:11 NCV

What You Want

"Treat people the same way you want them to treat you."

LUKE 6:31 NASB

Treating others the way we want to be treated is a measurable standard for loving well. If we are emotionally aware of how our actions make people feel, we will be thoughtful and kind. It's our responsibility to consider how our behavior affects those around us. When we realize there's a discrepancy between what we say and how we act, it's important to humbly embrace change.

Think about the way you desire to be treated. Do you long for someone to listen to you without judgement or cynicism? Do you want companionship that is loyal and thoughtful? Do you want your mistakes to be highlighted and your downfalls to be laughed at? The way you love others should reflect how you want to be loved. If you ask him, God will faithfully equip you to love well. It pleases him when his children treat each other with kindness.

Think of practical ways you can treat others with the respect and love you desire.

Above Reproach

Live honorable lives as you mix with unbelievers,
even though they accuse you of being evildoers.
For they will see your beautiful works and have a reason
to glorify God in the day he visits us.

1 PETER 2:12 TPT

Living an honorable life does not have to be complicated.
It means living with our values in line with God's nature.
We are honorable when we practice being honest, humble,
and accountable for our mistakes. We do our best to do the
right thing, and we make amends when we fail. We know
that grace equips us to live rightly, and mercy covers us
when we fall. We don't let pride get in the way of growth,
and we love others the way God has loved us.

You don't have to be perfect to be honorable. It is much
more important that you live in the light and are aware of
how your actions line up with Scripture. When you live
wisely and are teachable along the way, you will stand out
from the world. It is honorable and godly to admit when
you are wrong and be open to change.

What does living an honorable life mean to you?

Genuine Affection

*Be kindly affectionate to one another with brotherly love,
in honor giving preference to one another.*

ROMANS 12:10 NKJV

Through Christ, we have entered into God's family. As
family members, we should do our best to love one another
well. Scripture urges us to be kindly affectionate toward
each other. We are meant to do more than simply tolerate
each other. Our love should be genuine and thoughtful.
We are called to give preference to one another and to treat
each other with tenderness.

As a follower of Christ, love is at the center of all you are
called to. It isn't easy to bend to the preferences of others,
but it is what you are urged to do. If you find yourself
insisting on your own way and criticizing how other people
live, perhaps it's time for a heart evaluation. Ask God to
help you grow in love and he will gently steer you in the
right direction.

*Think of one or two ways you can show genuine affection
to others today.*

Liberated in Love

We have freedom now, because Christ made us free.
So stand strong.
Do not change and go back into the slavery of the law.

GALATIANS 5:1 NCV

Jesus purchased our freedom when he sacrificed his life and was resurrected from the grave. He saved us from the power of sin and death. We cannot become any more or less free. As such, we are meant to live in the fullness of all God intended for us. There is no need to walk in shame, despair, or guilt over our failures and mistakes.

You are no longer limited by your own capabilities. You don't have to strive for acceptance, forgiveness, or freedom. All of those things have been given to you without measure. When you allow yourself to be a slave to the law, it's like a painter holding a brush while insisting he doesn't have the right tool for the job. You have everything you need! Stand strong and remember that Christ has set you free.

In what area of your life do you desire freedom?

Marvelous Mercy

"Go and learn what this means:
I desire mercy and not sacrifice.
For I didn't come to call the righteous, but sinners."

MATTHEW 9:13 CSB

Mercy is better than sacrifice. God doesn't want our rituals or our carefully curated ways of living. He doesn't have a list of requirements we must meet for salvation, and he doesn't withhold his presence from us when we fail. This is the entire point of the gospel. Jesus came to set us free from a life bound by sacrifice and the law. We are free because of God's mercy.

God doesn't need you to present him with a perfect life. That's not what he wants from you. He wants you to know him, just as he knows you. He wants to have fellowship with you and for you to experience his peace and affection. He wants you to find satisfaction in his presence, and he wants you to see his goodness for all your days.

How can you embrace mercy over sacrifice today?

Compassion First

"You must be compassionate, just as your Father is compassionate. Do not judge others, and you will not be judged. Do not condemn others, or it will all come back against you. Forgive others, and you will be forgiven."

LUKE 6:36-37 NLT

It's easy to quickly judge those who offend, hurt, or irritate us. We like to create opinions of others and hold firmly to them. It takes less effort to create emotional distance than to put in the work of reconciliation. We aren't meant to take the easy way out. Compassion, forgiveness, and the hard work of relationships can be painful, but it is necessary and God honoring.

God has shown you incredible compassion. The right response is to show the same compassion to those around you. Loving God and others is your highest purpose. It often looks like offering grace and kindness when you would rather be critical or harsh. While judgement might feel good, it hardens your heart and keeps you separated from love.

How can you keep your heart soft when you would rather be critical?

Supernatural Strength

You armed me with strength for battle;
you humbled my adversaries before me.

PSALM 18:39 NIV

When we have nothing to offer on our own, God steps in to empower us in our weakness. When we cry out to him, he answers. We can always count on his help; all we have to do is ask. How many times have we felt abandoned or alone only to realize we didn't even ask him for help? If we haven't cultivated the discipline of running to God in our distress, we shouldn't be surprised by our frustrations.

God wants to strengthen you for the battles you face. He doesn't want you to stand against your enemies alone, and he doesn't want you to grit your teeth through trials. He is available and able to help you. You are not supposed to persevere on your own. Run to him when problems arise and let him help you. Surrender to his love and let him strengthen you for the journey you're on.

How has God armed you for battle in the past?

Trustworthy and Faithful

Commit your way to the Lord;
trust in him, and he will act.

PSALM 37:5 ESV

From the first time we knelt at the cross and committed our lives to the Lord, we began a journey of surrender. Our lives are no longer our own, but they are God's. We follow Jesus's example, and we do our best to honor God with our actions. We follow him, and he faithfully keeps his promises. We commit our ways to him, and he acts on our behalf.

Commit your way to the Lord. Acknowledge his sovereignty and give him authority over your life. Submit your plans and goals to him because he knows best. Walk steadily with him each day. When you come to a fork in your path, depend on his understanding over your own. He does not promise that your life will be free of suffering, but he does promise to be with you every step of the way. As you lean on him, he will fulfill his purposes for you.

Prayerfully commit your plans to God today.

Full Acceptance

You did not receive the "spirit of religious duty," leading
you back into the fear of never being good enough. But you
have received the "Spirit of full acceptance," enfolding you
into the family of God.

ROMANS 8:15 TPT

God doesn't want us to be trapped by feelings of obligation.
There isn't a list of requirements we must fulfill in order
to be deemed acceptable by him. Jesus died so we would
have a clear path to God's presence. When we use actions,
behaviors, or opinions to make ourselves feel successful, we
are essentially trying to add to the gospel.

Does following God feel like an item on your to-do list,
or is it rooted in a relationship that offers full acceptance?
Through Christ, you have been declared good enough.
You have been welcomed into the family of God. Your
actions cannot add or take away from what God has
declared. Instead of striving to be enough, relax into the
understanding that your acceptance has already been
determined.

How does feeling accepted impact
how you live out your purpose?

Open Your Hand

"The poor will not cease to exist in the land; therefore I am
commanding you, saying, 'You shall fully open your hand
to your brother, to your needy and poor in your land.'"

DEUTERONOMY 15:11 NASB

Scripture clearly says the poor will always exist. God doesn't
expect us to eradicate poverty. He does expect us to open
our hands in generosity whenever we can. As followers of
Christ, we are meant to notice the needy among us and do
whatever we can to alleviate their suffering. We should be
aware of our neighbor and willing to be generous when
needs arise.

God is generous, and he calls you follow his example.
Whether you are in a season of abundance or not,
generosity is possible. God hasn't given you a formula to
abide by or a quota to meet. Generosity doesn't hinge upon
the value of what you give. It's dependent on a soft heart
and a willingness to notice the needs of others. You can be a
cheerful giver no matter what your resources look like.

How can you grow in generosity today?

Good News

"The LORD has anointed Me
To preach good tidings to the poor;
He has sent Me to heal the brokenhearted."

ISAIAH 61:1 NKJV

Through Christ, we are set free and made whole. God's redemptive promise is fulfilled in Jesus. As was prophesied, Jesus has brought us out of darkness and into light. His love is our liberation, and his mercy is our means for communion with God. He brings restoration, redemption, and hope. Through him, we have been given a pathway to eternal life.

Jesus loves to heal the brokenhearted. He loves to set the captive free. He loves to give hope to those who are suffering and joy to poor in spirit. No matter how long you follow him, it is good to remember your desperate need for a savior. As you grapple with the challenges life throws at you, remember the miraculous simplicity of who Jesus is and what he has done for you. When you were broken, he healed you. When you were lost, he gave you hope.

Dwell on the good news of Christ's anointing today.

Listen and Apply

Truly happy people are those who carefully study God's perfect law that makes people free, and they continue to study it. They do not forget what they heard, but they obey what God's teaching says.

JAMES 1:25 NCV

The excitement of learning can quickly fade when we realize the amount of work required to apply what we've learned. If we only read God's Word, we will miss out on experiencing the fruit it could produce in our lives. Simply reading isn't enough. We are meant to carefully study it and obey what it says. Not only will we make wise choices, but Scripture says we will be truly happy if we study and apply God's law.

It's difficult to retain something if you don't put it into action. Instead of simply hearing the Word, take the necessary steps to obey it. Don't be overwhelmed by this task. You aren't meant to apply all of Scripture at once. Ask the Holy Spirit for discernment and he will lead you in the right direction.

What area of your life have you felt convicted to change?

Constructive Choices

"Everything is permissible for me,"
but not everything is beneficial.

1 CORINTHIANS 6:12 CSB

Just because something is excusable, doesn't mean we should do it. We each have free will and are fully capable of living how we see fit. We get to make our own choices, and there isn't technically anyone telling us what to do. Even so, the presence of freedom doesn't mean we should be cavalier with our behavior. It takes maturity and self-control to deliberately make wise choices.

It's important to pay attention to how your actions impact your life and the lives of those around you. Every decision you make has positive or negative consequences. If something doesn't serve your purpose or goals, don't give it your time or energy. With the help of the Holy Spirit, you can discern what types of behavior are best. Pay attention to the fruit of your habits and accept responsibility for your actions.

Have any seemingly harmless habits snuck into your life?

Blameless and Free

There is no condemnation for those who belong to Christ Jesus. And because you belong to him, the power of the life-giving Spirit has freed you from the power of sin that leads to death.

ROMANS 8:1-2 NLT

Through Jesus, we are free from condemnation. Even though we deserve a guilty verdict, we are given abundant mercy and grace. We don't have to carry doubt, shame, or fear of being misunderstood by God. We don't have to be afraid of impending punishment. He has removed all guilt and given us hope for what's to come!

If you bury yourself in guilt, you'll miss the abundant life that Jesus offers you. You are not meant to spend your days drowning in your mistakes. Lay aside your burdens because God has already liberated you. Don't take on shame or wallow in regret. Instead, let your guilt push you closer to God. He offers you complete freedom. Take him up on it! Live in the light of his mercy and embrace a life of repentance.

How does freedom from guilt allow you to fulfill your purpose?

Joyful Trust

The LORD is my strength and my shield;
my heart trusts in him, and he helps me.
My heart leaps for joy,
and with my song I praise him.

PSALM 28:7 NIV

Deep and abiding trust leads us to joy. When we believe God is in control and his love will always cover us, we can lay aside our burdens and experience the lightness that comes from trusting him. We don't have to fight, strive, and claw our way to happiness. We can fully lean on God's loyal love to carry us through life. As we trust him, he helps us, and our hearts are filled with gladness.

Your relationship with God is an ongoing cycle of surrender, faithfulness, and praise. You admit your need for God's strength, he faithfully shows up, and you glorify him for all he's done. Whether or not your circumstances change, God is worthy of your praise. He might not change the details of your life, but he will faithfully transform your heart and give you peace when you ask. He is your strength and your shield at all times.

How has trust led to joy in your life?

Teamwork

Plans go wrong for lack of advice;
many advisors bring success.

PROVERBS 15:22 NLT

We are not meant to be islands. No one is supposed to walk through this life alone. We were created with a need for community and fellowship. If we pridefully insist on walking alone, we are more likely to get lost. Instead, we should embrace the wisdom and input of others. When we humbly ask for help, we set the stage for success.

No matter what your purpose or goal is, there is wisdom in having many advisors. Ask for help when you need it and humbly acknowledge the ways other people contribute to your life. You might be capable on your own, but you are even stronger as part of a team. Not only do other people feel valued when you ask their advice, but you will benefit from having multiple perspectives to draw from.

How can you include other people in your plans today?

Hearts Revealed

Prove yourselves doers of the word,
and not just hearers who deceive themselves.

JAMES 1:22 NASB

We live out what we believe. It is inevitable that the depths of our hearts are revealed by our actions and attitudes. It's important to evaluate our habits, lifestyles, and choices. What do they say about us? What underlying beliefs do they reveal? We cannot hide our true intentions or beliefs for long. The best course of action is to let the Holy Spirit search our hearts and gently reveal any discrepancies.

There are likely areas in your life where your actions don't line up with what you say. Though this may feel like a formal accusation, you can approach these issues with curiosity. God is not ashamed of the things in your life that don't quite line up. He is committed to transforming your heart for all your days. He is constantly at work in your life. As you humbly surrender, he will faithfully lead you along a path of growth and abundant life. Don't be discouraged. God will gently and faithfully correct you if you let him.

*Shame inhibits growth. Trust God to deal
with your discrepancies today.*

Good Character

Those with good character walk on a smooth path,
with no detour or deviation.
But the wicked keep falling
because of their own wickedness.

PROVERBS 11:5 TPT

The book of Proverbs is full of examples of good character. As we read, we learn that wisdom goes hand in hand with integrity, honesty, and trustworthiness. If we are wise, we will do what is right and will value authenticity and high moral character. The rewards of loving wisdom are great. When we have good character, Scripture says we will walk on a smooth path.

Good character is developed by the daily choices we make. It's not something that happens overnight or without intention. In order to develop a good character, you must have the humility to admit when you are wrong. Without humility, you won't see a need for growth or change. When you willingly submit yourself to God and allow him to transform your heart, he will keep you upright. You won't fall when you walk with him hand in hand.

How has God transformed your character in the past?

Upholding Justice

"Keep justice, and do righteousness,
For My salvation is about to come,
And My righteousness to be revealed."

ISAIAH 56:1 NKJV

Promoting justice is a worthy use of our time. God, who is truly just, is always on the side of the oppressed. He lifts up the broken, and he tends to those who are hurting. He doesn't exploit the weaknesses of others, and he notices when someone is overlooked. These are qualities we should seek to embrace. If we want to display his character to the world, we must be willing to stand in the presence of injustice.

The world is full of suffering and despair. It can be incredibly disheartening to feel powerless in the face of corruption. Just because the imbalance is great, doesn't mean you should give up or stand idle. Instead, remember God is faithful. Maintain hope that one day everything will be made right. As you wait, keep your heart soft and ask God how you can take a stand when you see injustice.

How can you promote justice in your community?

Pursue Peace

Live in peace with each other. Do not be proud,
but make friends with those who seem unimportant.
Do not think how smart you are.

ROMANS 12:16 NCV

If we are devoted to the Prince of Peace, it is only right that
we pursue peace in our own lives and relationships. This is
a quality we don't see displayed in the world. Haughtiness,
personal gain, and dissension are often elevated above
the pursuit of peace. It is countercultural to actively work
toward reconciliation and humility.

While it's not wrong to be drawn to status, wealth, or
charisma, remember that God highly values those who are
unimportant. The world has its own standards of success,
but you aren't meant to live by the world's standards. It
is honoring to God when you notice someone who is
overlooked. It is pleasing to him when you set aside your
preferences for someone else. Let the Holy Spirit soften
your heart and give you a new longing for peace.

How do you actively pursue peace in your relationships?

Greatest Purpose

"I am the way, the truth, and the life.
No one comes to the Father except through me."

JOHN 14:6 CSB

We don't have to wander the world to find our purpose.
We don't have to struggle through dense forests or try to
navigate an impassable path. In Christ, we have all we need.
He is the way, the truth, and the life. The circumstances of
our lives and how we spend our days doesn't matter nearly
as much as our pursuit of Jesus. Our highest purpose is to
love him with everything we have. Any other pursuit or
desire must fall in line after what is most important.

Take a deep breath and remember that there is nothing
holding you back from accomplishing your greatest
purpose. You were made to have communion with God and
Jesus provides the only way for that to happen. The highest
level of satisfaction for your soul can only come from his
presence. You don't need more money, a higher education,
or different circumstances to attain what your soul needs
most. Nothing is holding you back from running to Jesus.

Have you placed your own goals above your greatest purpose?

Loving Rescue

I trust in your unfailing love.
I will rejoice because you have rescued me.

PSALM 13:5 NLT

We put our trust in God, and he is faithful to rescue us. He lifts us out of fear, sin, and shame. He generously offers us mercy and draws us into his presence. Even when we wander away from God's best, he faithfully meets us when we turn back to him. When we earnestly and humbly call upon his name, he rescues us. His loyal love lifts us from the ashes of yesterday's disappointment. He is the God who paves new paths in the wilderness and turns our biggest failures into opportunities for breakthrough and redemption.

There's a balance to be found between expecting God to do great things in your life and remembering that he has already done great things. He is your rescuer, and he has saved you. He has redeemed you from the power of sin and death. Through Jesus, God made a way where there wasn't one. When you put your trust in him, he lifted you out of a pit you could not escape! Rejoice because God is your deliverer!

Rejoice in something the Lord has done for you.

Persistent Hope

They will have no fear of bad news;
their hearts are steadfast, trusting in the LORD.

PSALM 112:7 NIV

The flood of disheartening news is incessant. Each day we hear of new atrocities and the prevalence of evil we cannot bear. If we are not careful, we may forget that amidst the breaking news there is also the presence of goodness, kindness, and mercy. God has not stopped working in the world. Even when it seems dismal, we can trust in his plans. We can root our hearts in his steadfast love and be encouraged by his faithfulness.

God remains your steadfast help both in times of peace and in times of trouble. His presence is more persistent than you can imagine. Therefore, your hope can also be persistent. God is with you and every other believer. He will not give up, and his purposes will not be thwarted. He will keep every one of his promises. Even when you get bad news, God is with you.

*Pay attention to what sparks fear in your heart
and give it to God.*

Always the Same

Jesus Christ is the same
yesterday and today and forever.

HEBREWS 13:8 ESV

Christ was with the Father in the beginning, before a word was spoken and the world was made. He walked the earth, was crucified, rose again, and is seated at the right hand of his Father. Through it all, he has never changed. We can rely on his consistency and steadiness. While the world shakes around us and even the seasons change, Jesus remains the same.

Jesus' character is reliable in a way you might struggle to comprehend. It's unlikely you've ever experienced anything truly consistent and steady. Even the healthiest relationship in your life has ups and downs. The steadiness of Jesus is the anchor for your soul. You can cling to him without wondering if his strength will wane or his mercy will run out. You can count on his love in every season of the soul. No matter how rocky or unpredictable your life becomes, Jesus is always the same.

How does the consistency of Jesus impact your pursuit of him?

Say Anything

Though He slay me,
I will hope in Him.
Nevertheless I will argue my ways before Him.

JOB 13:15 NASB

Job is a powerful example of devotion to God. Even when his circumstances were unfathomable, Job remained faithful. He refused to deny or disown his Creator. He was immovable in his faith, yet he wasn't afraid to be painfully honest with God. He pleaded and argued with him, and he let his raw emotions be seen freely. When we experience great heartache, we shouldn't be afraid to be honest before the Lord. We can be faithful and authentic at the same time.

God is not bothered by your emotions. He can easily handle your intense emotions. Brutal honesty can be very cathartic, especially when you feel like you have to be steady for the sake of others. You never have to do that with God. You can put your hope in him, and in the next sentence argue your case before him. There is room for it all in the grace of his presence!

Make time today to bear your soul to the Lord.

Generations of Faithfulness

Our fathers' faith was in you—
through the generations they trusted in you
and you came through.

PSALM 22:4 TPT

God always comes through. He is faithful to his people through every generation. Time does not limit him. Though culture, technology, and social systems change, God is always the same. He is not swayed by the shifting ways of the world. His faithfulness to our ancestors is just as great as his faithfulness to us. From the beginning to the end of time, God shows up for those who depend on him.

Be encouraged by looking at the past. Throughout history you'll see countless ways in which God has proven his faithfulness to his people. Hindsight is always clearer than when you are walking through a current struggle. Testimonies of God's goodness can carry you through your present heartaches. His loyal love has already been displayed in your life, and you can count on it to be displayed again.

*Make a list of God's faithfulness that you can revisit
when you are struggling.*

Motivated to Persevere

If we hope for what we do not see,
we eagerly wait for it with perseverance.

ROMANS 8:25 NKJV

As followers of Jesus, we have put our hope firmly in something we cannot see. There is evidence of his faithfulness all around us, but we cannot physically see Jesus working in our lives. Furthermore, we cannot see the finish line of the race we are running. We know that he will return and make all things right, but we cannot literally set our eyes upon that day. As such, everything we hope for requires faith and perseverance.

If it hasn't been already, your faith will surely be challenged. There will be a point in your life when you want to give up on what you believe. This is why it's so important to develop perseverance. With perseverance, you can withstand life's storms and remain faithful. As you look toward the fulfilment of God's promises, be hopeful and stay devoted to Jesus.

Why can you have hope for what's to come?

Always Content

I have learned to be satisfied with the things I have
and with everything that happens.

PHILIPPIANS 4:11 NCV

When we learn how to be satisfied with what we have, we
give ourselves the gift of emotional stability. There is great
peace to be found when we aren't consistently worried
about what we are missing. Instead of constantly comparing
our lives to those around us, we can focus on glorifying
God in our present circumstances. Our confidence should
come from God's faithful presence in our lives rather than
our ability to make ourselves comfortable.

Developing satisfaction in your present circumstances isn't
always exciting, but it is incredibly powerful. Cultivating
contentment gives you the freedom to focus on purpose
over fleeting satisfaction. When you have a deep connection
to God who never changes, you won't be distracted by
the ever-changing details of your life. Every day is a fresh
opportunity to lean into gratitude and connection rather
than disappointment and dissatisfaction.

Is your life defined by contentment or dissatisfaction?

Wait Expectantly

Be silent before the LORD and wait expectantly for him.
PSALM 37:7 CSB

We each have a calling and a purpose. Above all else, we are meant to love God and the people around us. It is difficult to flourish in the pursuit of those things when we are constantly discouraged by the choices of others. Scripture tells us not to be agitated when evil prospers. To put it blatantly, we have the freedom to mind our own business and let God handle it. Instead of fretting or being distracted by ways of the world, it's important to remember that God's victory will not be thwarted.

Have you ever lost sleep over what's happening in the world? Have your thoughts been consumed with worry over how so many horrible things can be happening at once? This is not God's intention for you. He wants you to put your trust in his plans. Quiet your heart before him and wait with great expectation. He will not fail. No matter how dark it seems, his light will shine through. Devote yourself to him, love those around you, and leave the rest in his hands.

How has agitation taken hold in your heart?

Reliable Messengers

An unreliable messenger stumbles into trouble,
but a reliable messenger brings healing.

PROVERBS 13:17 NLT

Trouble waits for us when are not true to our word. As
followers of Jesus, we should be reliable and trustworthy.
Our words matter and we should be mindful of how they
impact other people. We should follow through on what
we say and tell the truth in all situations. It is better to stay
quiet than to say something we don't mean or can't uphold.

Ask a few trustworthy people if they consider you to be
reliable and true to your word. Soften your heart and take
their words to heart. It takes courage to make room for
growth, and it isn't always comfortable. If you're unhappy
with their assessment, you have an opportunity to make a
change. Ask the Holy Spirit for help and try to change your
habits. Remember that God is on your side, and he will
joyfully help you develop good character.

What are some practical ways to develop reliability?

Faith to Believe

Without faith it is impossible to please God, because anyone who comes to him must believe that he exists and that he rewards those who earnestly seek him.

HEBREWS 11:6 NIV

God rewards those who earnestly seek him. When we faithfully pursue him, we can depend on his promise. Our search for him comes with a guarantee. We don't have to wonder if it will be worth it or worry that our efforts will go unnoticed. He sees our faith and he is pleased by it. As we acknowledge his existence and surrender our lives to him, he meets us with the fullness of his presence.

Have you overcomplicated your faith in the past? Remember that every time you approach God, you acknowledge his existence. Your pursuit of him, even when it feels weak, is an act of faith in itself. As you do your best to honor him, God is infinitely pleased with you. He sees every ounce of faith you possess. Your desire to fulfill your purpose for him does not go unseen. Every single time you point your heart toward him, God is proud.

Ask the Holy Spirit to show you where faith has led you already.

August

Many are the plans in a person's heart,
but it is the LORD's purpose
that prevails.

PROVERBS 19:21 NIV

Honorable Steward

It is required of stewards that they be found faithful.

1 CORINTHIANS 4:2 ESV

A steward looks after someone else's property or resources. Scripture says that we are stewards of the mysteries of God. We are meant to share the truth about who he is with the world around us. We should point people to him in love and be gracious as he is gracious. Our character should reflect his as we seek to follow his ways.

God has poured his loving kindness upon your life. He has been gracious with you, and he has given you mercy you don't deserve. As such, you can be a good steward toward others. You can boast in the work of the cross, and you can serve those around you with faithfulness and gentleness. You can represent God to the world by using your gives and talents to honor him.

How can you be a faithful steward
with what has been entrusted to you?

All Things

He who sits on the throne said,
"Behold, I am making all things new." And He said,
"Write, for these words are faithful and true."

REVELATION 21:5 NASB

God is the master restorer and redeemer. He can and will fix everything that is broken. There is no sorrow, grief, or trauma that God will not heal. One day, when Christ returns, we will experience the full perfection of God's goodness. He will mend everything that has been torn apart, damaged, or ruined. He will find everything that is lost. He will fill every dark shadow with his light, and he will bring eternal peace to our desperate hearts.

Perhaps there are many parts of your life that don't look how you want. Maybe you see the brokenness of the world and you feel distraught or discouraged. Don't let your hope die. Remember that a new day is coming. In his perfect timing, God will make all things new. He will keep each of his promises, and you will see all of creation restored to the glory it was intended for.

Where you feel stuck, lost, or broken,
invite God to bring renewal.

A Good Life

Life is good for the one who is generous and charitable,
conducting affairs with honesty and truth.

PSALM 112:5 TPT

Life is good when we conduct our affairs with honesty
because we have nothing to hide. We can go about our day
without wondering if we will be caught or found out. There
is freedom in having a clear conscience. Another aspect of
this is that being generous toward others brings personal
satisfaction and gratification. It feels good to be kind and
loving.

An open-hearted life is a good one. This doesn't mean
you won't have pain or difficulty, but if you are honest,
generous, and humble you will get through every season of
life with your character intact. God loves to teach you how
to live wisely and according to his character. He will help
you if you need to grow in generosity, honesty, or humility.

*Choose honesty and generosity in your dealings
and interactions today.*

Hold Fast

Let us hold fast the confession of our hope
without wavering, for He who promised is faithful.

HEBREWS 10:23 NKJV

Confident conviction is a powerful force. When we cling
to the one who is everlasting in love, faithful in truth, and
overwhelming in goodness, we will stay steady and secure.
We won't be tossed around by the storms of life because we
have assurance in the one who holds everything together.
Our hope remains intact despite circumstances because we
know God will keep his promises.

When you observe your life, do you see the ability to hold
fast without wavering? Do you feel steady when trials come,
or do you feel constantly behind and insecure? If you see
weakness or weariness in your life, don't despair! This is an
opportunity to rely on the strength of God. He will solidify
your faith if you ask him. Your inability to hold fast doesn't
disqualify you from his help. In fact, his strength is glorified
in your weakness.

*Today, let the Holy Spirit reveal your weaknesses
and trust in God's strength to uphold you.*

No Lying

God is not a human being, and he will not lie.
He is not a human, and he does not change his mind.
What he says he will do, he does.
What he promises, he makes come true.

NUMBERS 23:19 NCV

God has no need to deceive or manipulate. Everything he does is truthful and right. We can depend on what he says, and we can rely on his word. We can count on him to come through when we need him, and we can trust he will not abandon a single one of his children.

When you believe that God is honest and faithful, you set yourself up for success. You will encounter many trials, heartaches, and doubts throughout your life. Pain cannot be avoided, but if your trust cannot be shaken, you will stand firm no matter what. If you believe God keeps his promises, your hope will not waver in the fiercest storm.

*Speak today's verse over your life and ask God
to solidify your trust in him.*

Really Free

> "If the Son sets you free,
> you really will be free."
>
> JOHN 8:36 CSB

People who live with limiting beliefs often try to pull others down to their level. Why should you be so free when they are clearly not? Christ offers us all the same measure of freedom. There isn't a smaller portion for some and a larger one for others. If we have been set free by the Son of God, then the only thing that holds us back from living in the fullness of that freedom is ourselves!

In Christ, you are free from the power of sin and death. You do not have to be bound by your failures or stuck under the weight of your mistakes. There is mercy to start fresh, peace to keep your heart at rest, and joy to fill the depths of your soul. As you surrender yourself to Jesus, you open yourself up to experiencing the fullness of his goodness and the freedom of his love.

Ask God to help you embrace liberty in every area of your life.

In the Fire

"Look!" Nebuchadnezzar shouted. "I see four men,
unbound, walking around in the fire unharmed! And the
fourth looks like a god!"

DANIEL 3:25 NLT

When Nebuchadnezzar sent three men into the furnace,
there was no hope for their survival. Not a single
person expected the day to unfold as it did. Given the
circumstances, the outcome was obvious. It was a complete
miracle that these men not only survived but were
unharmed. God did not leave them even when all the odds
were stacked against them.

When you go through trials, you are not alone. God has
given you his Spirit, and he is your steady companion
and advocate. It doesn't matter where you go; he will be
with you at all times. You can take courage from the story
of Meshach, Shadrach, and Abednego. The same God
who delivered them also delivers you. You can put your
trust in him to see you through even the most impossible
circumstances.

*When you refuse to compromise, you can be sure that God
stands with you in the fiery trials that may come.*

Guardians of Goodness

Timothy, guard what has been entrusted to your care.
Turn away from godless chatter and the opposing ideas
of what is falsely called knowledge.

1 TIMOTHY 6:20 NIV

Timothy was anointed to teach and lead the church. When Paul wrote, encouraging him to guard what had been entrusted to his care, he wanted to be sure that Timothy would have confidence in the gifts he had. Timothy was young, and he needed encouragement and validation to stand strong. Paul urged Timothy to stay away from godless chatter and to focus on what he was called to do.

The world is full of distractions and idleness. You will be most fulfilled when you focus on what God has placed in front of you. Be faithful with the task at hand. Keep your eyes focused on what's in front of you and seek to embody the character of Christ in all you do. It might feel temporarily satisfying to quench the thirst of your flesh, but true gratification comes from being diligent and faithful with what God has given you.

How can you guard what God has entrusted you with?

Good Fruit

The fruit of the Spirit is love, joy, peace, patience, kindness, goodness, faithfulness, gentleness, self-control; against such things there is no law.

GALATIANS 5:22-23 ESV

There is no greater measure of our spiritual lives than the fruit of the Spirit. Fruit will grow where we tend it. When we yield our lives to the Holy Spirit and follow the wisdom of God's ways in our day-to-day lives, we will see much fruit. God's desire is that we would experience the fullness of all he offers. He wants your life to be full of good things as you follow the Spirit.

If you don't see godly fruit in your life, don't despair. It is an opportunity to readjust and ask God to mercifully help you realign. When you abide in Jesus, your life will produce the fruit of his Spirit. Abiding requires humility, obedience, and consistent fellowship. Don't ignore the importance of deepening your relationship with God and following his leadership every day.

Invite God into an area of your life that is barren of fruit.

Son of Righteousness

Do not get upset because of evildoers,
Do not be envious of wrongdoers.

PSALM 37:1 NASB

There are so many perceived benefits to doing the wrong thing. If we look at the external lives of people around us, it can seem like evil has some quick rewards. People everywhere are pursuing their own satisfaction and seem to be pretty happy about it. The world is full of injustice and if we focus on it, we will drive ourselves crazy noticing how wrongdoers are rewarded in this life.

Turn your eyes away from those who dishonor God. Stay steadily on the path he has for you and trust that he will justly reward all who follow him. Pursue goodness and you will not be forgotten. God sees everything perfectly, and he is an honorable judge. Just because you see evil rewarded now, does not mean the story is over. You can depend on God's ability to weave his plan together until all his promises come to pass.

How have you been discouraged over the state of the world?

Greatest Admiration

We can never look to men for help;
no matter who they are, they can't save us,
for even our great leaders fail and fall.
They too are just mortals who will one day die.

PSALM 146:3 TPT

There is no one on who can promise and deliver what God can. Even the best leaders make mistakes. They stumble, fall, and let us down. We must be careful not to idolize leaders or place our faith in their abilities. They are as human as we are. We set ourselves up for disappointment because they cannot possibly remain on the pedestals we create.

God is your greatest hope. He is full of truth, light, and love. He is faithful, just, and powerful. Though it is good to receive help from others, you cannot fully rely on another human. Whether a political, religious, or social figure, no one is meant to take God's place on the throne of your heart. He is the only one who will never disappoint you. He will never fail you, and he will always come through.

*Why should God be the recipient
of your greatest admiration?*

Follow Your Conviction

"Entreat me not to leave you,
Or to turn back from following after you."

RUTH 1:16 NKJV

Ruth dearly loved her mother-in-law, Naomi. She counted Naomi as closer to her than the family who had raised her. When Naomi told her daughter-in-law to return to her own family instead of following her to her homeland, Ruth would have none of it. Naomi was her family. She could not be convinced of any option but to follow her.

When you are full of resolve and passion, it does not matter what others say. You must follow your heart and your conviction. Commitment coupled with conviction is powerful. Examine your heart and take a look at what you are committed to. Where do you focus the majority of your time, energy, and resources? Submit to the Lord and he will guide you along the right path.

In what areas of life has your commitment wavered?

Pure Religion

Religion that God accepts as pure and without fault is this:
caring for orphans or widows who need help,
and keeping yourself free from the world's evil influence.

JAMES 1:27 NCV

We are supposed to care for those who are suffering and alone. Orphans don't have the covering of parents, and widows have lost the stability of their husbands. Refugees, addicts, and people who are abused or oppressed should be among our highest priorities as believers. When we care for the vulnerable, we reflect the power of God's love. He cares for the helpless and we should too.

As a believer, you are called to live differently than the world does. Instead of prioritizing wealth, success, or independence, you are encouraged to care for the most vulnerable members of society. God's heart breaks with the oppressed and yours should too. It's easy to cast judgment on the state of someone's life, but it's hard to lay aside your opinions and love in a sacrificial way. Let God soften your heart toward hurting people who cannot give you anything in return for your love.

How have you actively pursued true religion?

Master Builder

Every house is built by someone,
but the one who built everything is God.

HEBREWS 3:4 CSB

God is the great architect, wise engineer, and master craftsman of the entire universe. Everything we know, including all we cannot see, was built by God. Nothing in creation has been made without his wisdom and power. We serve the one who created everything out of nothing. Everything he's made declares his glory and reflects his character.

Your life is not an accident. God made you intentionally and with great love. His hands are at work in the details of your life. When you follow the wisdom of God, listening to his leadership and choosing to walk in his ways, you partner with him as his story unfolds. You are part of something much larger than yourself. Worship the one who made you for he is worthy of all your praise.

Look for evidence of God's goodness in creation today.

Treasures of Wisdom

The LORD grants wisdom!
From his mouth come knowledge and understanding.
He grants a treasure of common sense to the honest.
He is a shield to those who walk with integrity.

PROVERBS 2:6-7 NLT

There is so much wisdom in the counsel of the Lord. He isn't stumped by anything! He brings clarity when we are confused, and he brings understanding when we lack perspective. He gives common sense to those who are honest, and he protects those who have integrity. When we display godly character, he does not leave us empty handed. There is always a reward for doing the right thing.

God is happy to equip you. When you seek to do the right thing, he will help you. If your desire is to honor him, he will guide you and give you what you need. As you follow him, he will strengthen your character and build up your resolve. He will teach you how to live, and he will share the treasures of his understanding with you.

Seek God for the knowledge and understanding you need.

Help My Unbelief

Immediately the boy's father exclaimed,
"I do believe; help me overcome my unbelief!"

MARK 9:24 NIV

How many of us are like the desperate father we read about in Mark? We know Jesus can meet our needs, but we struggle to understand how it is possible. Jesus is so incredibly gracious with us. He takes our weak faith and meets us with incredible strength and mercy. He isn't annoyed by our doubts, and he doesn't hold back because we struggle to believe. Even when we aren't perfect, he shows up. He asks for trust over perfection.

Have you ever let your doubts get in the way of asking for help? Jesus doesn't expect you to believe perfectly. He knows your weaknesses and limitations. He is more interested in the state of your heart than in a display of spiritual strength. You can be honest with him. Tell him when you are struggling and invite him to strengthen your faith. He will meet you where you are and help you take the next step.

When you struggle to believe,
humbly admit your doubts to the Lord.

Declare Your Song

I will sing of steadfast love and justice;
to you, O LORD, I will make music.
I will ponder the way that is blameless.
Oh when will you come to me?

PSALM 101:1-2 ESV

David's praise starts out with a song about God's faithful love and powerful justice. He uses music to turn his heart toward the Lord. Through worship he acknowledges the endless wonders of God's character, and he presents his requests to him. He praises God for what he has done, and he cries out because he knows he needs him.

Worship is one of the best ways to communicate with the Lord. You can pour your heart out to him and simultaneously lift up his name. Through worship you gain the right perspective. You affirm God's greatness, and you declare your desperate need for him. This is how to keep your heart soft and contrite. The more you declare his goodness, the more your faith will be strengthened.

Lift a song of adoration to the Lord.

Great Confidence

If God has determined to stand with us,
tell me, who then could ever stand against us?

ROMANS 8:31 TPT

We've all felt like the odds are against us at some point. Life can be excruciatingly difficult. In the middle of trials or disappointments it's easy to feel alone and overwhelmed. However, it only takes a slight shift in perspective to realize we are not as alone as we may feel. The God of the universe is on our side. He is our strength when we are weak. He is our strong tower and our ever-present help in times of need.

If you have put your trust in God, he will faithfully stand with you. Whether you are tormented by a physical enemy, confused by doubt, or navigating grief, nothing will overcome you. Though you may experience great trials and seasons of pain, God is with you. He has pursued you and declared that you belong to him. He will keep your soul steady even if everything else falls apart. No enemy will prosper against the God who holds you firmly.

Do you feel secure in God's hands? Why or why not?

Walking Worthy

I, the prisoner of the Lord, beseech you to walk
worthy of the calling with which you were called.

EPHESIANS 4:1 NKJV

Paul often encouraged churches to get their priorities in
order. He encouraged them to live in a way that would
honor God. He wanted them to behave in a way that didn't
conflict with God's character. When he urges us to walk in
a way that is worthy of our calling, he is reminding us that
our actions should line up with God's desires. First and
foremost, God asks us to love each other. Everything we say
and do should fall under this directive.

You have been called by Christ to love your neighbor as
yourself. This means treating others with patience and
kindness. It means having humility in all your interactions
and refusing to put your needs above the needs of others.
To love others well you must be willing to help carry their
burdens even when you don't want to. By doing this, you
put action to the faith you profess.

How can you walk worthy of your calling today?

Controlled by Peace

Let the peace that Christ gives control your thinking, because you were all called together in one body to have peace.

COLOSSIANS 3:15 NCV

Our human tendency is to be controlled by our emotions. It's not uncommon for our actions to be dictated by how we feel at any given moment. It takes self-control and surrender to be controlled by the peace of Jesus. Instead of lashing out in anger, or shrinking back in fear, we are meant to cling to the anchor of Christ's peace. When our thoughts are controlled by peace we will make calm, wise, and intentional decisions.

Through Christ, God has freed you from being a slave to your whims. No matter how you might feel, you can lean on the peace of Jesus. His peace creates space for you to slow down and consider God's perspective before you move forward. Peace keeps you from being frantic, stressed out, and overwhelmed. Surrender your thoughts to God and let peace rule in your heart.

Invite the peace of God to fill your mind, heart, and body.

Chosen

Before I was born, God chose me
and called me by his marvelous grace.

GALATIANS 1:15 CSB

Each of us has been set apart by God and called by his grace. He is not aloof or disinterested in us. He was aware of us before we were even born. His eyes are turned toward his children, and he is delighted by each of us. He is a good father, and he will faithfully pursue us until the very end.

God sees you. He is aware of you, and he is not inconvenienced by you. He knows each of your hurts, and he longs to have a relationship with you. Of all the things you might doubt in this life, you don't need to doubt the love of God. It is consistent, perfect, and limitless. His love for you can be seen in his loyalty and his faithfulness. He chose you before you were born, and he will relentlessly pursue you all of your days. Respond to his call and be transformed by his love.

How do you feel intentionally loved by God?

Different Rules

Few of you were wise in the world's eyes or powerful or wealthy when God called you. Instead, God chose things the world considers foolish in order to shame those who think they are wise.

1 CORINTHIANS 1:26-27 NLT

God doesn't require us to have it all together to be used by him. In fact, he often calls upon those who are under qualified, weak, and foolish in the eyes of the world. The ways of his kingdom are not like the ways of the world. He doesn't operate under rules made by man. He looks beyond our definition of success or power and sees straight into the heart.

God desires your willingness and fellowship much more than your skills or qualifications. He isn't concerned with your achievements, wealth, or abilities. The most important thing you can offer God is a humble heart and a desire to follow his ways. He is strong enough to compensate for any weaknesses or limitations you might have. Don't despair over what you lack or brag about what you think you have.

Be encouraged by biblical accounts of God using weak yet willing servants.

Practical Love

If anyone has material possessions and sees
a brother or sister in need but has no pity on them,
how can the love of God be in that person?

1 JOHN 3:17 NIV

God delights in sharing. He is not stingy with his resources, and we shouldn't be either. When there are people in need among us, we have no excuse to withhold our abundance. When we realize that every good thing we have comes from God, we can hold it with open hands. Our willingness to share our resources directly correlates with our understanding of how we got them in the first place.

The way of love is generous and kind. You cannot accurately display Christ's love without being generous with the gifts you have. It is a privilege and an honor to help someone in need. Instead of thinking about how your resources will diminish, remember that God is sovereign over everything you have. Partner with him and readily share whatever you've been blessed with.

Do you have more than you need?
Offer the excess to someone who needs it.

Drawn In

> "No one can come to me unless the Father who sent me draws him. And I will raise him up on the last day."
>
> JOHN 6:44 ESV

God draws us to himself with kindness. He reels us in with gentleness, and he keeps us secure in his love. This is not a bait-and-switch situation. God is even better than we imagine him to be. He is full of loyal love, endless grace, and powerful truth. We are not brought into his family only to become slaves to his purposes. We are sons, daughters, and heirs to his kingdom.

There is freedom in knowing that God is the one who draws you. Even the beginning of your relationship is in his hands. He reaches out first. He pursues you. He offers love, redemption, and mercy. It is not your job to find God but to respond to what he has already done. Praise him for the way he has steadily loved you.

Remember all the ways God has been kind to you.

Living Hope

All praise to God, the Father of our Lord Jesus Christ.
It is by his great mercy that we have been born again,
because God raised Jesus Christ from the dead.

1 PETER 1:3 NASB

Our salvation is fully based on God's mercy. He made
a way for us to experience the power of new life in his
kingdom. Through Christ, he has redeemed us and brought
us into his family. There is no other way for us to obtain
righteousness other than through Jesus. God's mercy,
displayed through the death and resurrection of Jesus, is
our only hope.

Remember to praise God for the glorious things he has
done. It is not simplistic for your worship to be focused
on the cross. You don't need to move beyond it to a more
complicated spiritual truth. You could spend your whole
life at the cross and not a single day would be wasted. God's
merciful plan for redemption is full, complete, and worthy
of your daily devotion.

Today, praise God for the simple gospel.

Keep Running

I run straight for the divine invitation of reaching
the heavenly goal and gaining the victory-prize
through the anointing of Jesus.

PHILIPPIANS 3:14 TPT

We will inevitably move toward our gaze. When Jesus
remains our focal point, we will get closer to him with
each step we take. He is our goal and our prize. He is our
strength and our salvation. There is no greater purpose in
life than to strive to be closer to him each day. As we follow
in his ways, he reminds us of the Father's great love for us.

Set your sights on connecting with Jesus. No matter what
else is going on in your day, make a deliberate choice to
point yourself in his direction. Strive to be near him and
you will not be led astray. Set your face like flint and devote
yourself to the continuous pursuit of his presence. He will
not let you down.

How can you run toward your heavenly goal today?

Cry Out

In my distress I called upon the LORD,
And cried out to my God;
He heard my voice from His temple,
And my cry entered His ears.

2 SAMUEL 22:7 NKJV

Some of us struggle to ask for help. We have learned to take pride in how little we need others. This isn't the way of God. While the world values independence and a do-it-yourself mentality, God asks us to remain dependent upon him. He is the only one who can truly provide what we need. He sees us perfectly, and he always knows what is best.

Recognizing your lack doesn't mean you have failed. There is no weakness found in leaning on God's strength. Cry out to him and offer him your pain, hurt, and fears. He isn't put off by your neediness. In fact, he rushes to help when you call upon him. His ears are attuned to your voice, and he promises to respond to you.

Ask for help when you need it today.

True Identity

"I am changing your name from Abram to Abraham
because I am making you a father of many nations."

GENESIS 17:5 NCV

When God leads us, he doesn't only change our trajectory,
but he changes our very identity. He gives us a new name,
and he rewrites our story. We can trust him with the details
of our lives because he sees the entire picture. He sees each
of our days clearly, and he knows exactly what we need. He
calls us to follow him, and he equips us to do it well.

God created you, called you, redeemed you, and continues
to lead you. You are who he says you are. His perspective is
what matters most. No matter what titles you have carried
in the past, your identity in God is most significant. You are
his beloved child, and he is your faithful Father. He holds
your life in his hands, and you can trust him to guide you.

*How do the titles you assign yourself line up
with God's perspective?*

Wonderful Revelations

"Call to me and I will answer you and tell you great
and incomprehensible things you do not know."

JEREMIAH 33:3 CSB

When God is our counselor, we can be sure that the
wisdom we receive is reliable and trustworthy. We can run
to him in times of confusion or frustration and be confident
of his ability to help us. We can call out to him and know
that he will answer. He loves to share his heart with those
who seek him.

God speaks to those who listen. It is his delight to share
the wonders of his wisdom with you. If you ask, he will
faithfully share his heart with you. He is not hiding from
you, and he is not withholding knowledge or understanding
from you. All you have to do is approach him with a
humble heart and posture yourself to hear his voice.

How have God's revelations changed your life?

God's Values

This is what the LORD of Heaven's Armies says:
Judge fairly, and show mercy and kindness to one another.

ZECHARIAH 7:9 NLT

To the best of our abilities, let's be sure to not show favoritism to some while withholding opportunities from others. God asks us to judge fairly. It's important to be aware of our biases and to approach them with humility. When we recognize the flaws in our perspective, we can grow and change. Fairness, coupled with mercy and kindness, is what God desires.

When you show mercy, kindness, and thoughtfulness to others, you can be sure the love of God is at work in your heart. In a world that values loud opinions and passionate debates, it is countercultural to be gentle and fair with your words and actions. When others turn to accusatory language, easy insults, and negative speech, you can follow the Word of the Lord and focus on kindness in all situations.

*How do your interactions with others line up
with God's values?*

God With Us

The Word became flesh and made his dwelling among us.
We have seen his glory, the glory of the one and only Son,
who came from the Father, full of grace and truth.

JOHN 1:14 NIV

The birth of Jesus was not the beginning of his existence.
He has always been. He was present at the dawn of creation
with the Father and the Spirit. He left the perfection of
heaven, took on flesh, and dwelt among us. He experienced
the pain and sorrow that accompanies humanity, and he
gave us a path to redemption.

Jesus' life shows you what the Father is like. When he
walked the earth, he painted a picture of God's character
and how much he loves his children. He showed you how
to draw near to God, and he gives you hope for the glory
of what's to come. God could have chosen any path for the
redemption of mankind, but he mercifully sent his beloved
son. He sent him so that you would experience his nearness
and follow him to the foot of the cross.

What does Christ's life reveal to you about the Father?

September

Teach us to number our days,
that we may gain a heart of wisdom.

PSALM 90:12 NIV

Lifelong Learner

Learn to do good. Seek justice.
Help the oppressed. Defend the cause of orphans.
Fight for the rights of widows.

ISAIAH 1:17 NLT

Instead of being discouraged by the absence of what we want to see in our lives, we can be motivated to continue learning. We will never be perfect, yet there is so much to grow in during this life. As we take on the posture of lifelong learners, we don't hesitate to work on the weak areas of our character. Every day is an opportunity to grow in grace and to practice doing good.

In what areas of your faith do you want to grow stronger? Do you want to increase your patience with others? Do you want to practice being compassionate? As you follow the Lord and trust his leadership, he will continuously soften your heart and transform you into his image. Approach your mistakes with humility and seek to honor the Lord in all you do.

How does your life reflect God's standard for doing good?

All You Need

"The LORD your God has blessed you in all that you have done; He has known your wandering through this great wilderness. These forty years the LORD your God has been with you; you have not lacked anything."

DEUTERONOMY 2:7 NASB

God is a faithful leader. He led his people through the desert after he delivered them from captivity. In a cloud by day and a fire by night, he guided them through a wilderness they could not navigate alone. He opened up the heavens to rain down manna every morning, and he provided water in dry and desolate places. He was faithful to them in the unknown, and he will be faithful to us in our own wilderness seasons.

Though wandering feels aimless, it is not without purpose or fruit. When you don't see the purpose of what you are experiencing, you still have the presence of God. He will never leave you or forsake you. You can trust his goodness and faithfulness. He will always provide what you need when you need it. Just as the Israelites had all they required, so you will not lack anything as you rely on God!

Where can you see God's faithfulness shining through in your life?

Richness of Heart

It is better to have little
with a heart that loves justice
than to be rich and not have God
on your side.

PROVERBS 16:8 TPT

Earthly wealth does not last. We can't take it into eternity with us. Does this mean we should discard any responsibility when it comes to finances? Of course not! It does mean that financial wealth should not be our main motivator. There are far more important things than the accumulation of money.

If you serve God, you must esteem his values and treasures more than earthly wealth. While money might lead to personal comfort and satisfaction, godly character leads to eternal value. Remember that God will provide for your needs; you can stop striving for more. There is no amount of wealth that will make up for not having God on your side.

Whether you have a little or a lot, the treasures of God's kingdom are available to you.

Everlasting Kindness

"The mountains shall depart
And the hills be removed,
But My kindness shall not depart from you,
Nor shall My covenant of peace be removed."

ISAIAH 54:10 NKJV

The natural world is shifting and changing all the time. Tides rise and fall, weather patterns move across the surface of the earth, volcanoes erupt, and earthquakes change the topography. We cannot make the earth and its seasons stand still. Even so, there is something we can count on no matter what. God's kindness will never depart from us. His covenant of peace will never be removed.

God's mercy is everlasting. It was present in the beginning when God spoke the universe into being, and it remains just as powerful today. It doesn't change with the shifting seasons of the world, and it won't diminish as time passes. When you become overwhelmed by the lack of steadiness in the world, turn your heart toward God's kindness. Focus on his mercy because it is the one thing that will always remain.

How has God's kindness given you peace and assurance in times of transition and testing?

Full of Joy

Be full of joy in the Lord. It is no trouble for me
to write the same things to you again,
and it will help you to be more ready.

PHILIPPIANS 3:1 NCV

God's presence is filled with joy. He is overflowing with
it, and he wants us to share in his joy. Sometimes we tend
to focus on aspects of our spirituality that seem lofty
or worthy of pursuit. We get caught up in repentance,
righteousness, and accurate hermeneutics. It's important to
remember that we are also meant to be filled with joy! God
wants us to experience the contentment and satisfaction
that comes from living a joyful life.

There is no reason to limit joy in your life. Just as God
wants to provide you with healing, peace, and redemption,
so he wants to fill you with joy! Your relationship with
him is not meant to be serious or morose all the time.
Remember that he is the author of joy, and he wants you to
experience the fullness of what he offers you.

Where is there room in your life for joy?

Store It Up

My son, if you accept my words
and store up my commands within you…
then you will understand the fear of the LORD
and discover the knowledge of God.

PROVERBS 2:1-2,5 CSB

Our hearts reflect the nature of what we take in. As such, we should be wise about the counsel we seek, the advice we listen to, and the company we keep. Above all, our greatest influence should be God and his Word. His wisdom is full of life-giving fruit. As we store up his truth in our hearts, we will gain a treasure trove of wisdom to pull from!

You cannot ignore the importance of knowing God, of listening to his voice and following his ways. There are no shortcuts to his wisdom, and you will not gain understanding by accident. You have been equipped to faithfully cultivate a relationship with God. As you walk with him, his ways will become your ways. Nurture your relationship with him and listen closely to what he says.

*Ask the Spirit to reveal a piece of wisdom
you can store in your heart today.*

Simply Ask

If you need wisdom, ask our generous God,
and he will give it to you. He will not rebuke you for asking.

JAMES 1:5 NLT

It would be great if our loved ones could read our minds. They would know exactly what we want, and we wouldn't have to communicate our needs. Yet, it is not their responsibility to know what we expect if we have not communicated it. When we practice advocating for our needs, we set others up for success.

In the same way, you can practice asking God for what you need. While he already knows your heart, he wants you to deliberately seek him. Don't struggle on your own when you have access to the throne of God. Run to him and share your needs with him. If you ask him for wisdom, he promises to give it to you without holding back.

Where do you need God's help today?

Helpful Correction

Listen to advice and accept discipline,
and at the end you will be counted among the wise.

PROVERBS 19:20 NIV

When we resist correction, we end up hurting others and going down unnecessarily painful paths. There is freedom in humility because it allows us to adopt correction which leads to developing stronger character. Pride keeps us from knowing the wealth of wisdom that is available to us as followers of God.

God's correction is not controlling or shame inducing. He invites you to take ownership of your decisions and choose a better way. He mercifully allows you to be aware of your mistakes and also gives you a path forward. He builds you up rather than tearing you down. His correction is for your good, and his wisdom is helpful and clear.

How can you embrace correction in your life?

Careful Attention

Look carefully then how you walk, not as unwise but as
wise, making the best use of the time, because the days are
evil. Therefore do not be foolish, but understand what the
will of the Lord is.

EPHESIANS 5:15-17 ESV

Reaching our goals requires intentionality. If we don't take
agency over our decisions or look ahead to the goals we
want to achieve, we may never reach the destination we
desire. However, when we carefully look at how we walk,
we set ourselves up for success. Awareness makes room
for correction, repentance, and the application of godly
wisdom.

When you think about your purpose and your present life,
where are the disparities? Are you treating people the way
you want to be treated? Are you using your time wisely,
pouring into relationships as well as your personal growth?
Do you have a vibrant relationship with the Lord? You get
to choose how you walk through this world. As such, look
carefully at how wisdom can lead you today.

How can you live wisely today?

Return to Him

Return to your God,
Maintain kindness and justice,
And wait for your God continually.

HOSEA 12:6 NASB

Have you wandered far from where you once were in your relationship with God? No matter where you are on your journey, you can pivot and change directions. God's arms remain open and ready to welcome you. It is never too late to make a change for the better. As long as you have breath in your lungs, you can return to a wholehearted connection with your Maker.

God is always available to you. He desires a connection with you, yet he will not force you into it. It is your job to respond to his invitation. Return to him whether it's been years, months, or days since you last acknowledged him. He will not turn you away. As you turn your eyes toward him, he will meet you with mercy and grace.

Without shame, turn your heart toward God.

Where Wisdom Is

Where can wisdom be found? It is born in the fear of God.
Everyone who follows his ways
will never lack his living-understanding.

PSALM 111:10 TPT

Wisdom is born in the fear of God. This is because without the fear of God, we won't recognize who he is compared to who we are. If we don't acknowledge his greatness and our weakness, we won't see the need for wisdom. Through awe and adoration, we position ourselves to receive from God, fully knowing that without him we are lost.

Do you need wisdom in your life? The answer to that question should always be a resounding yes! Wisdom is not the kind of thing you can ever have enough of. If you think you have enough, perhaps pride or complacency has taken root in your heart. Like a gardener who faithfully pulls each unwanted weed, don't let pride create a home in your life. Embrace a life a worship and consistently acknowledge your need for God. Stand before him with humility and consistently pursue wisdom.

How can you actively pursue wisdom today?

Solid Foundation

"Whoever hears these sayings of Mine, and does them, I will liken him to a wise man who built his house on the rock."

MATTHEW 7:24 NKJV

We live in a society that is inundated with information. We can explore any topic without limitation or hindrance. This is even true with theology. We are no longer limited to a sermon once a week or a handful of commentaries. We can stand under the firehose of technology and saturate our lives in truth if we want. Unfortunately, hearing the truth consistently does not equate to living it out. It doesn't matter if we have memorized all of Scripture if we don't know how to apply it to our lives.

If you want to be a wise builder, you must take God's Word and apply it to your daily life. Before you get overwhelmed thinking about the discrepancies in your life, remember the Holy Spirit is your teacher and guide. Partner with him and he will lead you down a path that bears fruit and leads to eternal life. You don't have to frantically apply everything you've learned at once. Trust the Holy Spirit's leadership and build your house one step at a time.

How can you practically apply a biblical principal today?

He Never Tires

The LORD is the God who lives forever,
who created all the world.
He does not become tired or need to rest.
No one can understand how great his wisdom is.

ISAIAH 40:28 NCV

God's wisdom is far above the wisdom of this world. We don't even have a frame of reference for his intellect and understanding. His strength is more powerful than every military put together. There is nothing he cannot accomplish, and there is no limit to his understanding. He is the God who lives forever, and he doesn't grow tired or weary. His unending power is beyond what we can comprehend.

Though you grow tired often and easily, God never does. You can trust him because he never fails. Though your weaknesses are great, his power is greater. You can rely on him, rest in him, and have confidence in his ability to do what you cannot. Don't wear yourself out by trying to stay on top of every detail of your life. Commit your ways to him and trust his sovereignty.

Deliberately rest under God's watchful eye.

If You Must

"The one who boasts should boast in this:
that he understands and knows me—
that I am the LORD, showing faithful love,
justice, and righteousness on the earth,
for I delight in these things."

JEREMIAH 9:24 CSB

Scripture is pretty clear that boasting isn't a trait of the wise. People who glorify their strengths often overlook their weaker areas, hoping others will too. We all have strengths and weaknesses, and it shows maturity to embrace both with humility. Bragging about ourselves only reveals our insecurities while bragging about the Lord highlights his power in our life.

If you feel the need to boast or brag, boast about God. Tell others how faithful he has been in your life. Declare his righteousness over your own. Remember that your accomplishments carry very little weight in God's kingdom. He is far more concerned with the state of your heart than your list of successes. Ask the Holy Spirit to reveal areas of your life where pride has taken root and practice boasting in God instead of yourself.

Make a list of Godly boasts.

Be Present

Don't long for "the good old days."
This is not wise.

ECCLESIASTES 7:10 NLT

Nostalgia is a powerful force. It pulls us into the past and fills us with either longing or regret. There is nothing wrong with looking back and cherishing the former seasons of our lives. However, it isn't wise to focus more on what's behind us than what is to come. We should be wholeheartedly serving God in our current season. Longing for the past won't change our current circumstances.

Instead of longing for the past, take what you've learned and utilize it going forward. There are lessons to be gleaned from your previous experiences. Take those gifts and embrace the day you've been given right now. God has faithfully carried you up until this point in your life, and he will continue to do so. Don't miss out on what he has for you today by fixating on what has already happened.

Let go of your previous experiences and make room for God in your current season.

Best Efforts

Work hard to prove that you really are among those God has called and chosen. Do these things, and you will never fall away.

2 PETER 1:10 NLT

In today's passage of Scripture, Peter encouraged the readers to develop Christ-like virtues. By practicing these good deeds, they could prove their allegiance to God. In other words, the fruit of their lives was evidence that they were faithful followers of Jesus. When we live with self-control, patient endurance, and mercy, we reveal that the law of God's love is at work within our hearts.

Don't let the fear of legalism keep you from walking out in the life God has called you to. Working hard to prove that you are among those called by God is not the same thing as having a works-based mentality. Spend time in his presence, receive his generous mercy, and be transformed by his love. Your actions should reflect the miraculous redemption you have experienced. From the abundant grace God has given you, show the world what it looks like to follow Jesus.

Trust the Holy Spirit to transform your life one step at a time.

Never an Outsider

"Those who were not my people I will call 'my people,'
and her who was not beloved I will call 'beloved.'"

ROMANS 9:25 ESV

God is gracious to all who come to him. His family is not exclusive. He will not turn away from anyone who calls upon his name. There is nothing about us that disqualifies us from being welcomed into his kingdom. No matter our ethnicity, language, culture, or social status, we are all on equal footing before God. The world likes to categorize people and make clear divisions, but God sees all of humanity as his beloved children.

When you come to the Lord, you are ushered into his presence by his loving-kindness. If you've ever felt like an outsider, you know the discomfort of not belonging. It hurts when someone excludes you, whether it is intentional or not. There is no fear of rejection when it comes to God's family. He has made space for you, and you belong with him. Embrace his love for you and find confidence and comfort in his promises.

How can you welcome others as God has welcomed you?

Assigned to Love

As the Lord has assigned to each one,
as God has called each, in this way let him walk.

1 CORINTHIANS 7:17 NASB

Each of us should walk according to our calling. Scripture is clear that our highest calling is to love God and others. As such, everything we do should fall under those two categories. Though the details will surely differ, we are each meant to devote our time and resources to loving God and others. There is no purpose higher than this.

Don't get distracted by what others may or may not be doing around you. Keep focused on what God has given you to do. With the wise and gentle help of the Holy Spirit, you will stay on the right path. Commit your day to him and trust him to lead you. If you find yourself constantly worried about the details of your calling, remember the overarching principles God has asked you to embody.

*Keep your eyes on your own steps today
and find confidence in God's instructions.*

Breath of Life

Yahweh-God scooped up a lump of soil, sculpted a man,
and blew into his nostrils the breath of life.
The man came alive—a living soul!

GENESIS 2:7 TPT

God created all we know and see. In the beginning he
separated the waters from the heavens, and he created the
land and seas. He made all the flora and fauna, from the
smallest microbes to the largest living animals. He crafted
man and woman with love and intentionality. He breathed
life into his creation, and he declared that it was good.

You are alive because God has deemed it so. He is the
author of life and as such, he highly values it. Even on
your worst day, your very existence glorifies God. You are
the work of his hands. He sustains you, and he longs for a
relationship with you. You were created in his image, and if
you let him, he will guide you through all of your days.

How can you glorify your Creator today?

Revelations of Hope

I pray that your hearts will be flooded with light
so that you can understand the confident hope
he has given to those he called—his holy people
who are his rich and glorious inheritance.

EPHESIANS 1:18 NLT

The light of God shines on our hearts and illuminates our understanding of his goodness. The more we get to know him, the more we see how incredible his plan for redemption is. He is the God who finds the lost, fixes the broken, and sets the captive free. Every good thing he does during this lifetime points toward the glory of what's to come.

Let the promise of Christ's return fill you with hope. When life feels impossibly hard, remember a day is coming when everything will be made right. Though you grieve now, one day you will experience the fullness and perfection of God's kingdom. When your hope wavers, cling to what you know is true. Ask God to flood your heart with light and remind you of his faithful promises.

*Ask the Holy Spirit to fill you with anticipation
for Christ's return.*

Daily Opportunity

Why wait any longer? Get up, be baptized,
and wash your sins away, trusting in him to save you.

ACTS 22:16 NCV

When we have a revelation of the truth, we should seize it right away. When the opportunity for freedom arises, we shouldn't hesitate to take full advantage of it. A prisoner doesn't stand in front of an open door and wonder if they should walk through it. In the same way, we shouldn't overlook the glorious freedom Christ offers us. He stands in front of us with abundant mercy and grace. It's our responsibility to respond to what he has already done.

You can't change the past, and you cannot control what will happen in the future. All you have is the ability to respond to Jesus today. In this moment, you can turn toward him and surrender your heart. You can kneel at the cross and humbly declare his greatness. You can choose to honor him with the decisions you make, and you can experience the unending love he has for you.

How will you respond to Jesus today?

All We Need

His divine power has given us everything required for life and godliness through the knowledge of him who called us by his own glory and goodness.

2 PETER 1:3 CSB

Everything we need to live rightly is found in God. We don't have to go looking for answers outside of him. We don't have to prove ourselves worthy, score highly on an exam, or demonstrate our skills to qualify for godliness. Everything we need is given to us through the Holy Spirit. He is our counselor, teacher, advocate, and comforter. The strength and resolve we need is found in him. The tools we need to live a godly life are always available to us.

God is the source of everything you need. Not only does he love you extravagantly, but he equips you for each day you face. He knows every challenge you will encounter, and he is able to prepare you for it. You are never left alone to fight your battles. He is always with you and is able to help you every step of the way.

Give God any feelings of helplessness
and let him fill you with confidence.

Underlying Confidence

Many seek the ruler's favor,
but justice comes from the LORD.

PROVERBS 29:26 NLT

There are many who look for favor from powerful people.
If they have it, they feel valued, secure, and successful.
When our confidence comes from the affirmation of others,
we will never find true fulfillment. Instead of looking
to impress others, we should remember that God is our
highest authority. No matter how much power any human
possesses, God is the one in control. He is the one who
upholds justice and sustains all life.

While you should respect your leaders and treat every
human life with dignity, God is your highest authority.
Be careful not to place anyone on a pedestal higher than
him. Your actions should reflect devotion to him above all
else. Despite what the world might say, God's definition of
justice is true and right. Lean on him for discernment and
uphold his opinion above all others.

Whose favor are you seeking?

Blessed Assurance

Whoever loves God is known by God.

1 CORINTHIANS 8:3 NIV

Today's verse is simple in its message and powerful in truth. We don't have to wonder if God knows or loves us. If we love God, we can be sure that he knows us. Our devotion to him is a response to his unchanging character. He sees us, pursues us, and knows us fully. His commitment to us does not change. It's up to us to respond to the covenant he has made.

The blessed assurance of God's care and knowledge can provide security and confidence. You don't have to prove yourself to God, and you don't have to spend time explaining your motives or intentions. He knows you fully. He sees the depths of your heart, and he knows each of your thoughts. You can be yourself in his presence. There's no need to put up a front or try to impress him. Carry on with confidence knowing you are seen accurately and are fully loved.

Let God's knowledge of you bring you peace and security.

More Acceptable

To do righteousness and justice
is more acceptable to the LORD than sacrifice.

PROVERBS 21:3 ESV

God doesn't want our empty sacrifices or our rote rituals. He isn't impressed by outward shows of obedience that are devoid of any real connection. To do righteousness and justice is much more convincing of our devotion than any display of piety. The way we love others says more about our commitment to God than the principles or traditions we uphold.

How you live and love matters. God doesn't want you to live by the letter of the law but miss the entire point. Jesus' interactions with the religious leaders of his day made this very clear. You can do what is right according to the law and still be filled with corruption, pride, and hatred. It is much more important that your heart is at peace with God. Your action should reflect Christ's sacrificial love rather than your own ability to follow the rules.

How can you value righteousness and justice above sacrifice?

Make Space

Conduct yourselves with wisdom toward outsiders,
making the most of the opportunity.

COLOSSIANS 4:5 NASB

We should practice self-awareness and wisdom around
people who don't know us. This doesn't mean we put on
a fake persona, but rather we are gracious and deliberate
with what we say. When we are careful with our speech and
utilize self-control, we leave room for discernment. If we
are filling the space with our own opinions, we won't take
the time to listen well.

Grace empowers and equips you to love others well. Part of
this is being someone who listens wholeheartedly and isn't
always looking for the next opportunity to be heard. As you
develop the habit of being quiet, you'll notice you are more
aware of the needs and hurts of others. With awareness
comes the ability to practically love others the way Jesus
does. You can hear and respond in a way that brings dignity
and healing.

Practice listening well and speaking graciously today.

Embrace the Opportunities

We will show mercy to the poor and not miss an
opportunity to do acts of kindness for others,
for these are the true sacrifices that delight God's heart.

HEBREWS 13:16 TPT

Each day is filled with opportunities to embrace kindness.
If we want to practically apply what Scripture teaches, we
must develop an awareness of others and a willingness
to meet the needs we see. Putting the needs of others
before our own is a delight to God's heart. If something is
meaningful to God, it should be meaningful to us.

Practicing kindness takes discipline and dedication. The
more you actively look for ways to lift up others, the more
you will find them. If you are laser focused on your own
life, you won't have the wherewithal to notice what is
happening around you. Lift up your eyes and look beyond
yourself. This is countercultural in a world that exemplifies
feeling good and doing what you want. Instead of following
the world's example, follow Jesus' example of mercy and
kindness.

Ask the Holy Spirit to soften your heart
toward the people around you.

Pure Wisdom

The wisdom that is from above is first pure, then peaceable,
gentle, willing to yield, full of mercy and good fruits,
without partiality and without hypocrisy.

JAMES 3:17 NKJV

Wisdom is not an ambiguous quality that can't be defined.
The wisdom of God is easy to spot because Scripture
outlines it clearly. It is pure, peaceable, gentle, willing to
yield, and always has good fruit. God's wisdom reflects his
character. It is the embodiment of his love and the practical
application of his perfection. When we embrace living
wisely, we embrace the qualities of God himself.

Does your definition of wisdom line up with Scripture?
Stereotypically, you might see wisdom as being shrewd,
intelligent, and sage. Godly wisdom is those things, but it is
also willing to yield and full of mercy. These are aspects of
wisdom you might not see displayed as readily as others. If
you want to see wisdom's fruit in your life, remember that
God gives generously to all who ask.

Does the definition of wisdom surprise you?

Good Company

Spend time with the wise and you will become wise,
but the friends of fools will suffer.

PROVERBS 13:20 NCV

We've all been around old friends and noticed their many similarities. We've seen married couples who seem to communicate without words. The fact of the matter is, we become like the people we surround ourselves with. If we want to be wise we need to spend time with people who are wise. In the same way, we should be wary of the negative qualities of our closest friends.

Have you thought about how your friends influence you? Do you admire and respect the people who are in your closest circle? Ask the Holy Spirit to give you wisdom when it comes to who you spend time with. Just because you see a level of immaturity in someone doesn't mean you should cut them out of your life. It simply means to use discernment and be aware of how that friendship is affecting your character.

Do your friends have a positive impact on your life?
How can you have a positive impact on your friends?

Through Christ

"He has done everything well.
He even makes the deaf hear and the mute speak."

MARK 7:37 CSB

Everything Jesus did was exemplary. While he walked the earth, he perfectly executed the will of the Father. He took every opportunity to glorify God, and he never failed to show people the miraculous love God had for his people. If we want to understand who the Father is, we can simply look at how Jesus lived. His life is a clear picture of the character of God.

From Jesus, you can learn about God's character and his intentions. Jesus wouldn't have healed the sick or given sight to the blind if God didn't want him to. From this, you can surmise that God values healing and wholeness. You might see glimpses of this during your lifetime but without a doubt, full and complete healing is yours through Christ. When he returns, all who have put their trust in him will experience the fullness of his miraculous redemption.

How have you experienced healing in your life?

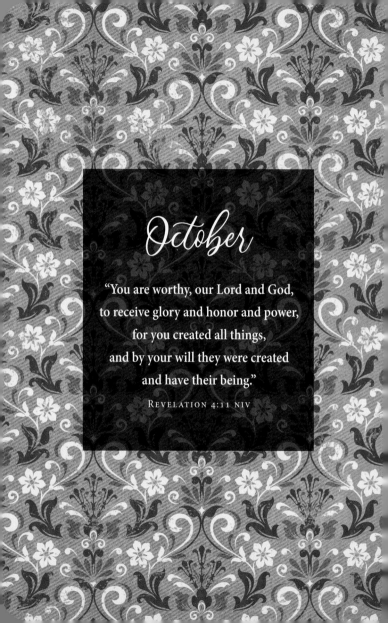

October

"You are worthy, our Lord and God,
to receive glory and honor and power,
for you created all things,
and by your will they were created
and have their being."

REVELATION 4:11 NIV

Different Standards

Listen to me, dear brothers and sisters. Hasn't God chosen the poor in this world to be rich in faith? Aren't they the ones who will inherit the Kingdom he promised to those who love him?

JAMES 2:5 NLT

God's kingdom doesn't operate like the world. Power and wealth don't impress him at all. He isn't biased or swayed by status. Rather, he has chosen to elevate the poor and lowly. What might be seen as weak or useless, God sees as immensely valuable. In eternity, he will more than compensate the poor for all they lacked in this life. God promises to give them his entire kingdom and all that is within it.

It is better to have a rich relationship with the Lord and an empty bank account than to have lots of wealth but no respect for God. When it comes to your purpose, don't let the world skew your idea of success. The truest success is found in a heart that is at peace with God and others; money can't offer that. Examine your heart and ask God to help you keep your priorities straight. He will faithfully lead you with gentleness and grace.

What is your measure of success?

Every Moment

You desired faithfulness even in the womb;
you taught me wisdom in that secret place.

PSALM 51:6 NIV

We each need God from the moment our existence begins.
We need his saving grace and loving wisdom to transform the
innermost parts of our being. He sustains, teaches, guides,
and protects us every moment of our lives. He doesn't do this
out of obligation or frustration. God delights in showing his
compassion to us. He is forever faithful and kind.

When you offer him your heart, he transforms you from the
inside out. You can trust him to receive you with mercy and
kindness. There is no mistake, failure, or fear that is too big
for him to handle. He wants to cleanse you from the weight
of your sin and give you freedom. Turn to him and he will
not forsake you. He will be faithful to you for all your days.
Nothing can stand in the way of his love for you.

*Bring your burdens to the Lord and turn your heart
toward him in repentance.*

Called to Go

By faith Abraham obeyed when he was called to go out to a
place that he was to receive as an inheritance.
And he went out, not knowing where he was going.

HEBREWS 11:8 ESV

God gave Abraham instructions that didn't make sense
at the time, yet he followed through on each promise.
Abraham stepped out in faith, and God equipped him to be
obedient. When God sets something within our hearts, we
can be sure he will do what is necessary to get us there. Our
job is to trust him and walk in the direction he is pointing.

Are you hesitating to take a step of faith? You don't have
to know the whole plan. All you have to know is that God
called you, so he will be faithful to you. As you move in
obedience, God will direct your steps. If he is your leader,
you have nothing to fear. Trust him, and he will do all that
he promised.

*Take a step of faith and believe God
will guide you along the way.*

What Matters

Neither is circumcision anything, nor uncircumcision,
but a new creation. And all who will follow this rule, peace
and mercy be upon them, and upon the Israel of God.

GALATIANS 6:15-16 NASB

In the early days of the church there was a divide between
Jewish and gentile believers. Some leaders wanted to
require circumcision for all new believers. In Galatians Paul
reminded the church that circumcision is not an issue at all
when following the law of Christ's love. What sets us apart
as believers is the grace, peace, and love we walk in. This is
what truly matters.

There are so many dividing issues in the church today.
Don't be distracted and lose sight of what Christ has
actually called you to. Ask the Holy Spirit to help you
discern when to speak and when to listen. Speak in a
way that lifts up others rather than prioritizing your own
opinion. This isn't always easy to do, but through the grace
of Jesus, you can love others with your words. Out of the
mercy you've received, you can pursue peace rather than
arguments.

*Ask God to soften your heart
and to focus on what matters most.*

You Decide

"Come and follow me, and I will transform you into men who catch people for God." Immediately they dropped their nets and left everything behind to follow Jesus.

MATTHEW 4:19-20 TPT

Jesus doesn't pitch himself like a salesman with ulterior motives. He does not manipulate us into following him, and he doesn't keep his intentions hidden. He is the way, the truth, and the life. He is clear about who he is and what he provides. It is our choice to follow him or not. He presents us with the truth and invites us to experience life the way it was intended. The invitation is open, and we get to respond according to our own will.

Each day you have an opportunity to respond to Christ's call. There is never a point when you are trapped, coerced, or made to do something you don't want to. He doesn't want you to feel obligated or overwhelmed. If you are beginning to feel weary in your faith, remember that Christ called you with the promise of abundant life, extravagant grace, and true rest for your soul.

Ask Jesus to renew your curiosity and wonder so that you might follow him with fresh desire.

The Best Example

The Son radiates God's own glory and expresses the very character of God, and he sustains everything by the mighty power of his command.

HEBREWS 1:3 NLT

Jesus is not dead. The cross did not overcome him. He is alive, and he sits at the right hand of the Father. While he walked the earth, Jesus revealed what the Father is like. Everything he did reflected the mercy and kindness of the Father. When we look at one, we see the other. The character of God and the actions of Christ are cohesive and cannot be separated.

When you are unsure of who God is, look to Jesus. If you need reassurance of his character or his intentions, look to Jesus. Look at his life, how he treated others, and what he spent time teaching. Without fail, Christ prioritized glorifying God's name, placing matters of the heart above outward actions, and lifting up the lowly. When you need guidance, look to Christ's example.

Ask God to help you follow in the footsteps of Jesus.

He Has This

Oh, Lord GOD, you made the skies and the earth
with your very great power.
There is nothing too hard for you to do.

JEREMIAH 32:17 NCV

Nothing is too hard for God. He made the skies and every corner of the earth. He created the molecular structure of every living thing. There is absolutely nothing he cannot do! When we remember who God is, our Creator and the sustainer of everything, we can rest in the knowledge of his unfailing faithfulness.

Whatever you are facing today, God can handle it. He is not stumped or unsure how to move forward. He is not overwhelmed by your trials, stress, or doubt! He is full of kindness, confidence, and power. Take a deep breath, steady your heart, and remember that he offers abundant peace in his presence. There is nothing to gain by stubbornly managing everything alone. Lean on him and let him carry your burdens.

*Lay your worries at his feet and rest knowing
that he is more than capable of helping you.*

Resurrection Power

"Go and make disciples of all nations, baptizing them in the name of the Father and of the Son and of the Holy Spirit, and teaching them to obey everything I have commanded you."

MATTHEW 28:19 NIV

This part of Scripture, known as the Great Commission, is perhaps one of Jesus' most memorable commands. We hear it a lot in the context of sending missionaries to lay their lives down in foreign countries. It's important to remember that Matthew 28 is applicable to everyone. The instruction to make disciples is not limited to working overseas or vocational ministry. Anyone with the Holy Spirit within them can teach others how to obey the commands of Jesus.

You have what it takes to make disciples. If you have surrendered your life to Jesus and are actively following his ways, you are fully equipped to encourage and teach others. It can be as simple as sharing what you've learned and glorifying God for what he's done in your life. If you have been transformed by God's mercy and grace, you are more than qualified to share it with those around you.

How can you help fulfill the Great Commission right where you are?

Joyful Justice

Justice is a joy to the godly,
but it terrifies evildoers.

PROVERBS 21:15 NLT

If we live in the light of God's ways, we have nothing to fear regarding his justice. While those who thrive in corruption will have to face the consequences of their ways, there is no shame in walking in integrity. There is no impending punishment for those who live according to Christ's law of love.

God's justice is better than the justice of the world. You can't always depend on your perspective or opinion. God is the only one who sees each situation clearly and without bias. It's important to rely on God's definition of justice over your own. With a soft heart and a willingness to be wrong, you can humbly submit your ways to his sovereignty. There is freedom in knowing that God is a perfect judge, and you don't have to be.

Seek to live in the light and leave justice in the hands of God.

Powerful Kingdom

The kingdom of God is not a matter of talk but of power.

1 CORINTHIANS 4:20 NIV

We've all met someone whose actions don't line up with their words. Their words might sound great, but they lack follow through. God does not work this way. He isn't like those among us who persuade us with grand speeches and emotional ploys. Everything he says is reliable and true. He has proven his faithfulness, and we can trust that he will continue to keep his promises.

God doesn't expect you to follow him simply based on what is said. The physical evidence of his glory is everywhere. His power is displayed in countless ways. You can see his hand on all of creation and in every good gift in your life. You've likely witnessed his provision and his care. Everything he says is backed up by a display of his mercy, power, and glory.

Where have you seen the power of God at work?

All Things

"With man this is impossible,
but with God all things are possible."

MATTHEW 19:26 ESV

There is so much that we are unable to do. We are limited by our humanity and individual weaknesses. Even our greatest strengths will not last the span of our lifetime. There are boundaries we must operate within and situations that are completely out of our control. Though the concept is difficult to grasp, God has no limits. There is nothing beyond the scope of his power.

Take a look at your life and try pinpoint the things you can actually control. Surely, it won't be a very long list. There is so much out of your hands, yet you have the ability to acknowledge the one who is in control. With God, all things are possible. His power at work in your life is your greatest asset. There is no need to rely on your own strength when you have access to the mighty power of God.

Today, surrender your impossible situations to God.

Gentle Wisdom

Who among you is wise and understanding? Let him show by his good behavior his deeds in the gentleness of wisdom.

JAMES 3:13 NASB

Wisdom is not harsh or demanding. It is not cold or cruel. Wisdom from the Lord is meant to be gentle and kind. It is gracious and full of mercy. Wisdom always reflects God's character, and it is never contradictory to his nature. If we seek wisdom, our lives will reflect the goodness of God. We will be led to live in a way that honors him and displays his love for the world around us.

If you want to live wisely, ask God. He will generously give you all you need. He promises that he won't hold back wisdom from those who seek it. True wisdom is humble, kind, and full of grace. The wisdom of God does not shrink back from the truth, but it also doesn't shame, manipulate, or brag. It is full of gentleness, peace, and patience.

How can you display the gentle wisdom of God?

Elevated Ways

"As high as the heavens are above the earth,
so my ways and my thoughts are higher than yours."

ISAIAH 55:9 TPT

We are limited in mercy. We are restricted in our capacity
to offer grace to others. God, however, is not. He does not
have any limits. His ability to shower us with mercy and
grace is beyond our understanding. There is nothing we
need that he cannot supply. When we humbly submit our
lives to him, he graciously bestows unending goodness
upon us.

There is freedom in understanding that God's ways are
higher than yours. His great wisdom and power allow you
to throw off your burdens and let go of your cares. You can
be completely free because he is perfect, and he promises
to take care of you. Submission to God is not restrictive or
disempowering. Instead, you can run to his mighty arms
and experience the perfection of his mercy and grace.

*How have you recently acknowledged
that God's ways are higher than yours?*

Straight to the Heart

The word of God is living and powerful, and sharper than any two-edged sword, piercing even to the division of soul and spirit, and of joints and marrow, and is a discerner of the thoughts and intents of the heart.

HEBREWS 4:12 NKJV

The Word of God is living and powerful. Every single word is necessary and valuable. If we have devoted our lives to following him, we must properly prioritize Scripture. It allows us to learn about God's character, and it equips us to live in a way that honors him. God's Word is a deep well that satisfies the longings of our soul. We can draw from it in times of draught, and we can depend on it to faithfully point us back to the Father's heart.

If you have ever felt pierced by the truth in Scripture, you have known the power of God's Word at work. His Word brings clarity, understanding, wisdom, and encouragement. It teaches you how to live, and it fills you with hope and endurance. God has given you his Word so you may experience his mercy and grace. Ask God to soften your heart and give you understanding as you read his Word.

How has the Word of God impacted you lately?

Humble Wisdom

Fools think they are doing right,
but the wise listen to advice.

PROVERBS 12:15 NCV

Scripture warns us that it is foolish to live with pride and arrogance. Fools think they already know everything they need to know. They don't listen to advice or value the input of others. When we refuse to acknowledge alternate points of view, especially if we are inexperienced, we are the ones who miss out. Pride says that we can do everything alone, but wisdom says that we need a community of support.

Pride can keep you from listening to good advice. No matter how intelligent or experienced you are, you need the input of others. When you humbly ask for help, you set yourself up for success. Each of God's children display various aspects of his character, and when we work together, we see a more accurate picture of his goodness. If you want to make wise choices, consider the fact that your opinion is not superior to anyone else's.

Ask God to soften your heart and give you ears to hear the opinions of those around you.

Timely Reminders

I will always remind you about these things,
even though you know them and are established
in the truth you now have.

2 PETER 1:12 CSB

We all need to be reminded of the truth. Sometimes life steadily progresses, and we forget the simple truths that our faith is founded upon. It's always a good idea to listen to reminders when they come. It is also good practice offering wise reminders to others. At the end of the day, we cannot hear the truth enough times. In our humanity, we are fickle and prone to wander. None of us are above the need for consistent reminders.

A timely word is like honey; it is sweet to the taste. Even if you've heard it several times, it never hurts to be reminded of God's love and grace. While it is good to dive into deep theological truths, it is also good to relish in the simplicity of the gospel. You don't have to reinvent the wheel by coming up with new ideas all the time. Just because you have already learned something doesn't mean that your soul can't be refreshed and rejuvenated by basic truths.

What is a simple truth you haven't thought about
for a long time?

Gracious Mercy

God is so rich in mercy, and he loved us so much,
that even though we were dead because of our sins,
he gave us life when he raised Christ from the dead.

EPHESIANS 2:4-5 NLT

God's mercy is a gift. It is not something that we have to strive for or earn. We are not required to prove ourselves worthy before we approach him. Jesus is the door to the Father. We come to him as we are, with open hearts, and he welcomes us into his kingdom with endless mercy and grace. He removes our rags and clothes us with the glory of his own nature. It is only because of Christ that we can experience the fullness of God's presence.

No matter how unworthy you may feel, God has chosen you as his own. He doesn't ask you to clean yourself up before you approach him. God is fully aware of your weaknesses and downfalls. He does not hold them against you. Instead, he provides a way for you to be free of your burdens. As you surrender to Jesus, he relieves you of your inequities, and he gives you the freedom to approach God with confidence.

Take a deep breath and stop striving.
Lay down your burdens and accept God's grace.

Unhindered Worship

Then I heard every creature in heaven and on earth and
under the earth and on the sea, and all that is in them, saying:
"To him who sits on the throne and to the Lamb be praise
and honor and glory and power, for ever and ever!"

REVELATION 5:13 NIV

One day, all of creation will offer their praise to the Lamb
of God. Every knee will bow, and every tongue will confess
that Jesus is Lord. We can look forward to this day with
great anticipation and delight. Imagine the immense
feelings of wholeness and satisfaction we will all experience.
There will no longer be anything holding us back from
wholeheartedly worshipping the one who is worthy of all
our praise.

There have probably been times in your life when you have
struggled to worship. You may have been distracted by your
own thoughts or even consumed by worry or fear. When
Jesus returns, the cares of the world will no longer be a
factor. Every trial, sin and distraction will be removed, and
you will worship God completely unhindered.

*Ask God to fill you with anticipation
as you look toward Christ's second coming.*

Humble Hearts

Humble yourselves, therefore, under the mighty hand of
God so that at the proper time he may exalt you,
casting all your anxieties on him, because he cares for you.

1 PETER 5:6-7 ESV

It is good to maintain a posture of humility before the Lord.
When we remain open to his instruction, correction, and
leadership, we make room for the freedom he generously
offers. He is a good leader, and we can trust him to care for
us. When we pridefully resist his guidance, we set ourselves
up for disappointment and unnecessary pain.

Keep your ears attuned to God's voice and fix your eyes on
him. Remember that his ways are higher than your own. You
can submit to him because he is worthy of your praise, and
he promises that he will not lead you astray. His commands
are not empty or without a firm foundation. If he says he will
exalt you at the right time, he will surely do it.

Cast your cares on him and rest in his mighty hands.

Spiritual Battles

Though we walk in the flesh, we do not wage battle according
to the flesh, for the weapons of our warfare are not of the
flesh, but divinely powerful for the destruction of fortresses.

2 Corinthians 10:3-4 nasb

As God's children we must recognize that the ways of this
world are not the ways of God's kingdom. We are called to
see beyond our earthly perception and see each situation
as he sees it. This means that sometimes we must set aside
what feels natural and embrace what is supernatural. As we
humbly follow Jesus, he will give us eyes to see.

It's important to remember what's at stake in the battles
you fight. As you embrace God's perspective, you'll see
there is more going on than you might realize. While you
probably won't engage in many physical fights during your
lifetime, your spirit will be tested continuously. Ask God to
strengthen your spirit so that you might stand strong in the
presence of your enemies. When temptation comes your
way, or the enemy poses a threat, God will be faithfully on
your side.

Ask God to give you greater spiritual awareness today.

Wait and Prepare

"I will send the fulfillment of the Father's promise to you, so stay here in the city until you are clothed with the mighty power of heaven."

LUKE 24:49 TPT

After Jesus was resurrected, the disciples were tasked with sharing the gospel with all who would listen. They were given a mission to share the good news across the world. God did not ask them to do this and then leave them empty handed. He wanted to equip them and fill them with power. He wasn't going to send them out unarmed and helpless, so he asked them to wait. They were told not to leave until they were clothed with the mighty power of heaven.

God will always give you what you need to accomplish his purposes. He does not give you a task and expect you to muster up the resources you need. He always equips his children to walk in his ways. He is a fair, just, and empowering leader. If God has called you to do something, you can be confident he will give you what you need. You can depend on his Spirit to direct you each step of the way.

If you are in a season of waiting,
trust that God is preparing you for what's next.

Never Fading

"The grass withers, the flower fades,
But the word of our God stands forever."

ISAIAH 40:8 NKJV

There is nothing on earth that will last forever. Seasons change, new life is born, and death inevitably claims many victims. We are all very familiar with this cycle. Even our very lives are subject to a beginning and an end. It is all we know. Yet, the Word of the Lord is beyond our understanding. It will last forever. Its poignancy will never fade, and it will never lose value.

You can put your hope in the Word of God. When you cannot depend on anything else, his Word is steady and reliable. It cannot be shaken, overturned, or denied. When everything else has withered and died, God's Word will stand strong. If you feel unsteady or lost, fasten yourself the anchor of God's promises. There is nothing that can overcome the King of your heart.

Dwell on a truth that has carried you through life's storms.

Living Freely

In the past, the law held us like prisoners, but our old selves died, and we were made free from the law. So now we serve God in a new way with the Spirit, and not in the old way with written rules.

ROMANS 7:6 NCV

When we walk in the love of Christ, we are liberated from the letter of the law. There used to be rules and requirements for pleasing God. There were sacrifices made and even then, a select few experienced his presence. Sin held us back from being with him, but Jesus has set us free from the restriction of the law. His perfection has granted us entry into God's glorious presence.

Through Christ, you are accepted and welcomed into the family of God. Christ died for you in the midst of your sin, not after you cleaned yourself up from it. While it is good to follow God's standards for your life, rules and restrictions are not what grant you entrance into his kingdom. Your faithfulness does not procure grace. Instead, take the abundant grace you've been freely given and serve God faithfully.

Ask God to reveal any areas of your life in which you're bound to rules.

Seek Maturity

Everyone who lives on milk is inexperienced with the message about righteousness, because he is an infant. Solid food is for the mature—for those whose senses have been trained to distinguish between good and evil.

HEBREWS 5:13-14 CSB

As we grow in our relationship with God, we move from immaturity to maturity. Godly maturity looks different from worldly maturity. It isn't defined by age or independence. Biblical maturity is defined by the ability to distinguish between good and evil and by an understanding of righteousness. When we continuously recognize that our righteousness comes only from Jesus, we will grow in our faith. As we fill our hearts with the knowledge of the Word, we will gain the ability to distinguish good from evil.

Spiritual maturity takes time and experience. The more time you spend in God's presence, the more you will grow. The more you fill your mind with truth, the more you will know how to live. Maturity does not happen overnight. It takes diligence and effort.

Ask God how you can practically move toward maturity today.

Represent Jesus

Whatever you do or say, do it as a representative of the Lord Jesus, giving thanks through him to God the Father.

COLOSSIANS 3:17 NLT

When we say we are followers of Jesus, our actions reflect upon him. We represent him to the world. Our words and behavior should be an accurate depiction of his character. This might feel like a heavy burden, but we have abundant grace to draw from. God has given us everything we need to live in a way that honors him. He readily heals our brokenness, and he mercifully teaches us how to follow his ways.

Whatever you do today, do it as a representative of Jesus. Love others the way he loves you. Forgive others the way he forgives you. Be gracious to others the way he is gracious to you. If you feel a discrepancy between your behavior and the character of Jesus, humbly ask for help. Repent of your wrongdoing and let the Holy Spirit lead you toward what is right. God is delighted by a heart that is willing to grow.

Ask the Holy Spirit to show you if there are areas your behavior should change.

By the Spirit

Walk by the Spirit,
and you will not gratify the desires of the flesh.

GALATIANS 5:16 NIV

We live in a world that prioritizes gratifying the desires of the flesh. Everywhere we turn we are told to pursue our own happiness at any cost. Our culture's guiding force is the unashamed pursuit of what feels good. This is not how we are meant to live. While gratifying our flesh might provide momentary satisfaction, it is not lasting or reliable. Without fail, we will find ourselves on a never-ending search to satisfy an unquenchable thirst.

When you follow the Holy Spirit instead of your flesh, you will find true satisfaction for your soul. God's presence is life-giving and eternal. The joy you find there will last forever. The peace you find there will never fade. God offers you far greater treasures than anything your flesh might crave. Today, lay down your desires and ask God to align your heart with his.

Which desires of the flesh have you been searching for?

Aim for Restoration

Aim for restoration, comfort one another,
agree with one another, live in peace;
and the God of love and peace will be with you.

2 CORINTHIANS 13:11 ESV

If we're honest with ourselves, how many of our interactions can be defined by a desire for restoration, comfort, peace, and agreeability? These are all things we should strive for in our relationships. When our goal is to pursue these things, God promises he will be with us. When we do our best to live in peace with each other, we honor the way God wants us to live.

Arguments and bitterness will keep you at a distance from those around you. You don't have to be close friends with everyone, but your interactions should always be kind and peaceful. It's not right to delight in drama, unkind debates, or conversations that create dissension. Instead, focus on restoration and honoring each other the way God asks you to.

*Practice pursuing restoration and peace
in your relationships today.*

Never Overtaken

No temptation has overtaken you except something common to mankind; and God is faithful, so He will not allow you to be tempted beyond what you are able.

1 Corinthians 10:13 NASB

Though the details may differ, we will all face temptation at various points in our lives. No one is immune, and we all have areas in which we are prone to compromise. We are not promised a life without struggle. We are promised that God will be with us every step of the way. He will give us a way to move forward no matter what sirens are calling our name. He equips us to stay faithful and endure the trials we face.

Let your heart be rooted in the Lord and depend on him every day. When temptation inevitably comes, he will guide you through it. He will give you the strength to persevere. When you come out on the other side, you will be stronger. Your faith will be bolstered, and you'll be reminded of how God is your ever-present help in times of need.

Do you believe you are equipped
to be victorious in the face of temptation?

Limited Time

Help us to remember that our days are numbered,
and help us to interpret our lives correctly.

PSALM 90:12 TPT

Today's verse isn't meant to give us anxiety. We don't need
to fret or worry about wasting time. God's commands are
not meant to layer burdens upon our shoulders but to
equip and guide us. As such, it is wise to recognize we have
limited time, energy, and resources. If we let him, God will
guide our steps and help us use our time well.

When it comes to managing your time, it's incredibly
helpful to know what season you are in. With a clear
vision and purpose, you can take deliberate steps each day.
When you interpret your life correctly, you will be able to
say yes or no to the appropriate things. You'll know what
is valuable and what isn't. There is a wealth of wisdom in
properly prioritizing your life.

Ask God to give you a vision for this season of your life.

Cast Your Cares

Give all your worries and cares to God,
for he cares about you.

1 Peter 5:7 nlt

When you withhold your thoughts from the Lord, you're inhibiting the opportunity for healing and growth. He already knows what you think, and he doesn't want you to carry your burdens alone. God cares for you more than you can imagine. You can give him your worries, your questions, and your fears. He won't be offended. He is more patient than you realize.

God invites you to cast all your cares on him. He knows you, and he wants to take care of you. He can handle the weight of your darkest thoughts. He can alleviate the heaviness you have from holding your hurts inside. Surrender to his love and let him show you how gentle and kind he is. Lay your cares at his feet and let him give you strength.

How have you been trying to carry your worries alone?

Like Jesus

Let everyone see that you are gentle and kind.
The Lord is coming soon.

PHILIPPIANS 4:4 NCV

Gentleness and kindness are not weaknesses. When we deliberately embody these qualities, we follow in the footsteps of Jesus. It doesn't cost us anything to be kind. It's as simple as smiling when we interact with people and paying attention to the needs of others. Gentleness can look like choosing our words carefully and showing up when someone is in pain. It can look like setting aside our opinions or wants in favor of someone else's.

Both gentleness and kindness are fruit of the spirit. This means when you are led by the Holy Spirit, you can trust him to prompt you toward gentleness and kindness. If you let him, he will show you opportunities to love others the way Jesus loves them. He will teach you when to speak and when to listen. He will guide you and help you live in way that exemplifies the character of Christ. God does not instruct you to act a certain way without equipping you to do so.

How can you embrace gentleness and kindness today?

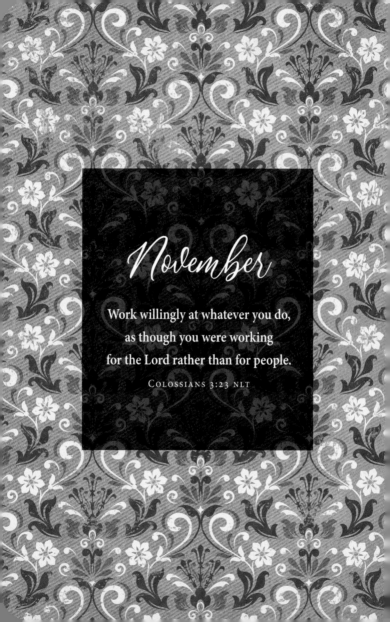

November

Work willingly at whatever you do,
as though you were working
for the Lord rather than for people.

COLOSSIANS 3:23 NLT

All Your Praise

Yours, LORD, is the greatness and the power and the glory and the splendor and the majesty, for everything in the heavens and on earth belongs to you.

1 CHRONICLES 29:11 CSB

As we enter into a month focusing on thanksgiving, let's turn our hearts to the one who owns the cattle on a thousand hills. He is the one who put breath in our lungs, set the stars and planets in motion, and lovingly draws us to himself. He is worthy of all our praise and devotion. Every good gift we have comes from him.

God shines brighter than the sun. He is more glorious than the most exquisite sunset. He is better than the best moments of your life. He is full of goodness, beauty, and power. He is full of kindness, grace, and peace. He is wonderful, and his glory will never cease. Turn your heart toward him and exalt his name!

What is your favorite way to offer God praise?

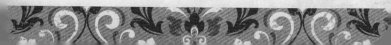

Chosen Words

A truly wise person uses few words;
a person with understanding is even-tempered.
Even fools are thought wise when they keep silent;
with their mouths shut, they seem intelligent.

PROVERBS 17:27-28 NLT

When we choose our words wisely, taking our audience into account, we practice self-control. We cannot read minds, so when we keep our mouths shut no one will know what we actually think about an issue. It takes diligence and discipline to master this skill. We are tempted to make our voices heard, but this isn't always the best way to communicate.

Self-control allows you to slow down and mindfully choose how you approach certain situations and challenges. It helps you be thoughtful about what you participate in and what you walk away from. Words have the power of building up others or tearing them down. It's important to choose your words wisely. If you are in the habit of speaking without thinking, ask the Holy Spirit to help you grow in patience and wisdom.

*Today, be mindful of your words
and how they might impact others.*

Delightful Satisfaction

Take delight in the LORD,
and he will give you the desires of your heart.

PSALM 37:4 NIV

God promises us the desires of our hearts. He doesn't say he will give us the desires of our flesh. God isn't giving us a free pass for whatever we want at any given moment. Instead, he fills the deepest longings of the human heart. In him, our desire to be loved, noticed, cared for, and valued is satisfied. In him, we find a sense of belonging and purpose. These are needs that cannot be fully met in any other way. We were made to commune with our Maker.

When you delight yourself in the Lord, your heart becomes enthralled with his goodness. When you depend on God's faithfulness, every gift he offers becomes an additional reason to give him your gratitude and affection. When you turn your heart toward him, he joyfully offers you the goodness of his presence and the bounty of his kingdom. Delight in who he is and trust that he knows exactly what you need.

Cultivate a heart of thanks as you remember who God is and what he has already done for you.

Cultivate Contentment

For the sake of Christ, then, I am content with weaknesses, insults, hardships, persecutions, and calamities. For when I am weak, then I am strong.

2 CORINTHIANS 12:10 ESV

Circumstances don't dictate contentment. We can be in the middle of a great trial and still be satisfied by the presence of the Lord. In 2 Corinthians Paul spoke about his personal cultivation of satisfaction in Christ. No matter what he was going through, he experienced the goodness of Jesus. His faith wasn't dependent on his own strength or ability to control his life. Instead, he knew that anything negative gave him a greater opportunity to depend on the Lord's strength.

When you are weak, God is strong. Lean on his grace to empower you when you have nothing left to give. When your capacity is low, he is unchanged. Instead of focusing on the trials you face, turn your attention to the presence of God. He is always near, and he longs to help you. He offers strength and peace no matter what you are going through.

If you have been discouraged by trials lately, remember they can draw you closer to God.

Every Corner

He loves righteousness and justice;
The earth is full of the goodness of the LORD.

PSALM 33:5 NASB

The earth is full of the Lord's unfailing goodness!
Everywhere we turn we can see evidence of his glory.
Every corner of the earth speaks to his gracious love
and meticulous care. From the beauty of a sunrise to the
intricacy of each ecosystem, God's goodness is evident. He
made everything with wisdom, and he holds it all together
with power and love.

You cannot run from God's presence. He is everywhere,
filling each corner and crevice with his light and love. You
are never far from him, and he is never out of reach. You
might feel as though there is a distance between you, but it
is never too big to cross. He is always near, and he invites
you to experience the depths of his goodness.

Look for signs of God's goodness
and rejoice in all he has done for you.

Love Gift

By grace you have been saved by faith. Nothing you did could ever earn this salvation, for it was the love gift from God that brought us to Christ! So no one will ever be able to boast, for salvation is never a reward for good works or human striving.

EPHESIANS 2:8-9 TPT

None of us can earn salvation. There is nothing we can do to prove we are good enough or to outrank someone else. There is no pressure to perform, and there is no list of requirements we must meet. Every qualification to be welcomed into God's kingdom has been met by Christ's death and resurrection. He has done all the work, and we reap the great and eternal reward.

Lay down your burdens and rest in the work that has been done for you. Your salvation is safe and secure in the hands of God. There is nothing you can do to earn a greater measure of it. May your desire to do good come only from the immense grace that has been showered upon you. Your salvation is not a reward but a loving and generous gift from your heavenly Father who cares for you.

When insecurity threatens you, remember that your worth in Christ is established.

Each Step

You have need of endurance,
so that after you have done the will of God,
you may receive the promise.

HEBREWS 10:36 NKJV

Life is full of beginnings, middles, and ends. While fresh starts are exciting and reaching a goal is motivating, the messy middle is where we need the strength to keep putting one foot in front of the other. We must cultivate the discipline of persevering even when we don't want to. If we make it to the end, we win. The longevity of our faith matters more than doing everything perfectly along the way.

Be encouraged today! Even by reading this devotional you are practicing turning your heart toward God! You're doing a good job. Keep putting one foot in front of the other. A life of faith is built one day at a time. In Christ, you have access to the grace of God which empowers you. When you are weary, remember that the strength you need doesn't come from yourself but from God.

*Today is enough. Take each step as it comes,
leaning on the Lord for stability.*

Take Captive

We capture every thought
and make it give up and obey Christ.

2 CORINTHIANS 10:5 NCV

We don't have to believe everything we think. Our thoughts can be fickle, selfish, and downright wrong. Just because something crosses our minds, doesn't mean it should impact our actions. Our thoughts are not indicative of our character or the strength of our faith. We are not enslaved to them, and we don't have to be discouraged by them. We have the ability to take our thoughts captive and submit them to Jesus.

It's unlikely that every thought you have aligns with Scripture or has a positive impact on your life. There may be cultural norms, old belief systems, or even traumatic events that have influenced you. Any number of things can have an impact on how you think. This is why it is good to practice the discipline of controlling your thoughts instead of being controlled by them. Submit your mind to the Lord and let him transform the way you think.

How do you redirect your thoughts when necessary?

In Everything

Rejoice always, pray constantly, give thanks in everything;
for this is God's will for you in Christ Jesus.

1 Thessalonians 5:16-18 csb

It is a good to cultivate gratitude in our hearts every day.
It takes diligence and intentionality to focus on what is
good. It's much easier to pay attention to our problems and
weaknesses. If we do that, we will quickly be discouraged
and disappointed. Instead, we can practice thankfulness.
As we look for reasons to give thanks, we will notice them
everywhere. If we are constantly looking for negativity, we
will also find it everywhere. We will find what we seek.

No matter what you are going through, there are glimpses of
goodness to be found. It's not always obvious, but in every
situation, there is an opportunity to be thankful. Having
an attitude of thanksgiving doesn't mean you are without
grief, disappointment, or pain. It simply means that you
can recognize the bigger picture even when difficult things
happen. By God's grace, you can be thankful amid trials.

Make a list of everything you are thankful for today.

Goodness Overcomes

Don't let evil conquer you,
but conquer evil by doing good.

ROMANS 12:21 NLT

Forces of evil are present in the world around us. We don't need convincing of this. The world is full of violence, hatred, and corruption. There are systems and people who manipulate others for their own gain. As followers of Jesus, we are called to conquer evil by doing good. We cannot individually overturn corrupt governments or rescue every person in danger, but we can do our part to spread the redeeming love of God everywhere we go.

You can incorporate doing good into every aspect of your life. The way you treat people, how you speak, and how you conduct yourself can display God's love for the world. You have daily opportunities to do good. Your actions matter, and while you may feel small, you can have a big impact simply by loving your neighbor. Join in God's work and do good in your own sphere of influence.

*Think of one good think you can do today
and commit it to the Lord.*

Life-giving Wisdom

The one who gets wisdom loves life;
the one who cherishes understanding will soon prosper.

PROVERBS 19:8 NIV

When we seek wisdom, we gain clarity and confidence. When our lives are devoted to displaying the wisdom of God, we humbly submit ourselves to his ways. We cannot pursue wisdom while pridefully holding on to our own perspective. Instead, we must be willing to see the world from God's point of view. He is the only one who can grant us knowledge and understanding.

Wisdom in itself requires humility. You must be willing to admit you don't have all the right answers to life's problems. Without humility, you will never seek wisdom because you won't even notice the need for it. There is freedom and life in seeking wisdom because the pursuit of wisdom requires you to ask God for help. When you ask him for help, he will wholeheartedly equip you to live rightly.

How can you cultivate the practice of seeking wisdom?

Take Caution

One who is wise is cautious and turns away from evil,
but a fool is reckless and careless.

PROVERBS 14:16 ESV

We are each in control of our decisions. Some of us may have a predisposition toward certain behaviors but none of us are without excuse. Scripture is clear that we are able to turn away from evil. It shows maturity when we take responsibility for our own behavior. If we want to be wise, we will act with caution and be aware of how our choices impact us and those around us.

Wisdom will never steer you wrong. Giving careful attention to your decisions will help you stay on the right path. When you make decisions remember that you always have a choice between what is right and wrong. It might take diligence and practice, but thoughtful behavior will only have a positive impact on your life.

*Choose the way of wisdom and pay close attention
to your decisions today.*

Sacrifices of Praise

Let's continually offer up a sacrifice of praise to God,
that is, the fruit of lips praising His name.

HEBREWS 13:15 NASB

We don't have to feel a certain way to praise God. In fact, it can be more powerful when we offer our praise despite how we feel at any given moment. When we choose to worship, we deliberately lift our eyes from our situation and focus on God. When we turn our attention toward him, he will faithfully meet us and transform our hearts.

This doesn't mean you have to fake your emotions or hide how you feel. God is comfortable with however you approach him. He already knows what's in your heart, and he isn't intimidated or bothered by any of it. Instead of letting your emotions keep you from approaching God, remember that you can confidently offer him your praise in every season of the soul.

Let your praise be based on who God is
instead of how you feel.

Oasis

"Are you weary, carrying a heavy burden? Come to me.
I will refresh your life, for I am your oasis."

MATTHEW 11:28 TPT

An oasis provides refreshment in the middle of the desert.
It's a place of refuge that stands alone in the midst of an
unforgiving and dry place. Jesus is our oasis. He offers us
rest and refreshment in the middle of life's harshest climates.
When we are dry, weary, and burdened, he invites us to
come to him. He is an oasis of life-giving peace. He offers
living water, refreshing nourishment, and rest for our souls.

When life feels harsh and impossible, let Jesus be your
refuge. His mercy and grace are exactly what your desperate
soul needs. Lay your burdens at his feet and let him refresh
you from the inside out. He doesn't want you to wander
helplessly through the desert. Instead, he wants you to
experience the renewal and hope only he can offer.

Give your burdens to Jesus and let him refresh your soul.

Be Still and Know

"Be still, and know that I am God;
I will be exalted among the nations,
I will be exalted in the earth!"

PSALM 46:10 NKJV

When we quiet our hearts before the Lord, we find a reprieve from the chaos in the world. Life presents us with many challenges, yet we always have a refuge available. We can lean on God's steadiness no matter what trials we face. When we surrender to him, he provides us with peace and true rest.

Each day, you can practice quieting your heart before the Lord. You can command your soul to patiently trust in his promises. Regardless of your feelings, you can posture yourself before God in humility and trust. As you lean on him for strength, he will lift you up and encourage you. He will sustain you and prove that he is faithful. You will never regret putting your hope in the Lord.

Quiet your heart and mind before the Lord today.

Acceptable Actions

We are trying hard to do what the Lord accepts as right and also what people think is right.

2 CORINTHIANS 8:21 NCV

From the grace we have been freely given, we should do our best to do what is right before the Lord. When we love him wholeheartedly, our behavior will reflect his character. We do not strive for goodness out of a sense of obligation, but we are honored to live rightly because of what Jesus has already done for us.

God has equipped you to live in a way that honors him. He has given you all the tools you need, and he is always ready to pick you up if you stumble. He doesn't expect perfection, and he is well aware of your weaknesses. He is eternally gracious with you, and he knows exactly how to help you. Follow him closely and expect that he will faithfully transform you into his likeness.

How can you honor God with your actions today?

Trust Him

Let those who suffer according to God's will entrust themselves to a faithful Creator while doing what is good.

1 PETER 4:19 CSB

When we walk in the path of God's purposes, it doesn't mean that we get a free pass from pain. At some point in our lives, all of us will know the sting of suffering and the heartbreak of grief. This doesn't mean our faith has failed. When the pain is too much to bear, let us turn toward the Lord. He is not disappointed by our weaknesses. Rather, he longs to lift up and encourage those who suffer.

God is trustworthy and faithful. He is our comforter, teacher, and friend. You never walk through seasons of suffering alone. He is with you through every painful experience. He sees every loss, and he knows the depth of your grief. When pain washes over you, his love washes over you even more. He is close to you, and he will comfort you if you let him.

How have you known God as your comforter?

Blessings over Curses

Bless those who persecute you.
Don't curse them; pray that God will bless them.

ROMANS 12:14 NLT

When someone hurts us, it takes self-control to manage our reaction. We are called to submit our desire for retaliation to the Lord. Scripture reminds us to bless our enemies and those who hurt us. This isn't easy and it can only be done by the grace of God. If we ask, he will clothe us in compassion and give us his perspective.

You can trust God with the most painful and unfair situations in your life. You don't ever have to worry about being forgotten or overlooked. He isn't asking you to ignore your pain or stuff your feelings away. He is asking you to trust him to handle what you cannot. He is the only one who can be truly just and kind.

Ask God for the grace to bless those who hurt you.

Confident Expectation

Faith is confidence in what we hope for
and assurance about what we do not see.

HEBREWS 11:1 NIV

We put our faith in various things each day. We trust the sun will rise and set. We believe that our heart will beat steadily. We don't doubt that the rain will come, and we know eventually the wind will blow. If we can confidently trust in each of these things, then surely, we can confidently trust in the Maker.

You exercise your faith every day without even realizing it. Think about all the things you depend on. God is the author behind it all. If you pay attention, you will quickly realize that every aspect of your life proves God is faithful and has always sustained you. Ask him to show you the ways he has shown up for you.

*Let God's faithful provision give you assurance
that he will continue to keep his promises.*

Do Your Best

Do your best to present yourself to God as one approved,
a worker who has no need to be ashamed,
rightly handling the word of truth.

2 TIMOTHY 2:15 ESV

We cannot achieve perfection, but we can faithfully do
our best. This is different than earning our place in God's
kingdom. He isn't asking us to strive for salvation, but he
is showing us the right way to live. By his grace, we are
equipped to continuously grow and mature. It is not vain or
prideful to seek to grow in faith, love, and humility.

If you want to rightly handle the word of truth, start by
immersing yourself in the Word. Take every opportunity to
fill your heart with God's instructions. He is your faithful
helper. He will steadily lead you along the right path, and
he will pick you up when you fall. As you do your best
to apply Scripture to your life, God will equip you and
strengthen you.

How can you apply Scripture to your life today?

Help the Weak

"In everything I showed you that by working hard in this way you must help the weak and remember the words of the Lord Jesus, that He Himself said, 'It is more blessed to give than to receive.'"

ACTS 20:35 NASB

Following Jesus means sacrificially loving others. We joyfully serve others because Jesus laid his life down for us. We give freely and generously to those in need because Jesus gave everything for us. We help the weak without frustration or resentment because Jesus met us at our weakest and lifted us up. In all things, we seek to be givers because of the abundance that we've been given.

The love of Christ isn't about words or nice ideas. It is practical and powerful, and it makes a difference in the lives of those who receive it. Following Jesus often looks like giving up your time, energy, and resources for the sake of others. This is rarely easy or convenient. It takes thoughtful intentionality to notice someone who is weak and reach out to help.

Today, keep your eyes open for those who are vulnerable.

Faithful in Prayer

Be faithful to pray as intercessors
who are fully alert and giving thanks to God.

COLOSSIANS 4:2 TPT

Prayer is a powerful way to connect to the Lord. It is also a practical way to help others by interceding for their needs. When we lift up the needs of others, we invite God to manage situations we aren't capable of handling. Our hearts are transformed through prayer, and our thoughts become more aligned with his perspective. His compassion softens our hearts and helps us see others the way he does.

There will be times in life when the only action you can take is to pray. This does not mean you are helpless or unproductive. Intercession is arguably the most productive thing you can do in any situation. Through prayer your heart will remain anchored in hope when your circumstances seem impossible. As you commune with your Maker, he will remind you of his faithfulness and strengthen you in times of weakness.

What is your first response in desperate situations?

Eternal Victory

Thanks be to God, who gives us the victory
through our Lord Jesus Christ.

1 CORINTHIANS 15:57 NKJV

There isn't a circumstance in this life that can keep us from
the love of God. No matter what we experience on earth,
we are promised victory through Jesus. While our suffering
may be great, we trust that one day everything will be made
right. Jesus' death and resurrection gives us eternal security
that cannot be taken away.

Of all the things God has done for you, the victory you have
through Jesus is the greatest. There is no physical treasure,
circumstantial favor, or answered prayer that compares to
the eternal gift of salvation. Through the ups and downs of
life, it's tempting to judge God's faithfulness by the details of
your days. Instead, worship God for the redemption he has
secured for you.

Ask God for fresh appreciation for your salvation.

Wholehearted Love

Love the LORD your God with all your heart,
all your soul, and all your strength.

DEUTERONOMY 6:5 NCV

We each have different talents, goals, and preferences. Our paths look different, and the way we spend our days varies from person to person. Despite this, we share one common purpose. We are meant to love God with everything we have. He is supposed to be our highest priority. Above all else, we were created to worship the one who formed us.

Do you love the Lord with all your heart, soul, and strength? This question isn't meant to cause shame but to remind you of what is most important. Loving God isn't supposed to be another item on your to-do list. Give him everything you have because he loved you first. Let your devotion be a response to what he has already done for you. Give yourself to God wholeheartedly and be transformed by the love he has for you.

How can you wholeheartedly love God today?

Sing to the Lord

I will praise God's name with song
and exalt him with thanksgiving.

PSALM 69:30 CSB

Music is a powerful way to connect to God. It transcends
language and reaches the deepest parts of our soul. When
we turn our thanks into praise, singing out of the depths
of our gratitude, we present God with a sweet offering.
Through worship we align ourselves with him and
deliberately look beyond our circumstances.

God is always worthy of your praise. There is never a
shortage of reasons to worship him. If you take the time to
quiet your heart, you will begin to notice that your life is
bursting with reasons to be thankful. Every good thing you
experience is straight from his hands. Praise him by telling
him everything you are grateful for. Even on your worst
days, there is reason to lift up his name.

Put on your favorite worship song and offer God your praise.

Great Peace

Those who love your instructions
have great peace and do not stumble.

PSALM 119:165 NLT

When we love God's instructions, we don't hesitate to put them into practice. We know everything he says has a purpose and is intended for our good. We trust him to see and understand everything we cannot. As we are obedient to him, we find great peace and a sense of security which cannot be found anywhere else. He directs our steps, and we rest knowing he is in control.

Following God's instructions is the best path for you. It will have a positive impact on your life and the lives of those around you. God's standards are not for your detriment or so he can control you. In his sovereignty, he knows what is best. It only makes sense to humbly submit to his wisdom. As you follow his ways, you'll experience the peace that comes from knowing you are secure in his hands.

How can you develop love for God's instructions?

Called to Freedom

Do not use your freedom to indulge the flesh;
rather, serve one another humbly in love.

GALATIANS 5:13 NIV

Jesus gave his life in exchange for our freedom. It cost him greatly, yet he counted us worthy of the sacrifice. His death and resurrection have given us eternal security. Without him, we would be lost in sin, guilt, and shame. Instead, we are forgiven and considered blameless. Our response to the freedom we've been given is supposed to be loving others in humility. We are not supposed to take our freedom and do whatever we want.

The entire law is fulfilled by loving others. There is no calling, instruction, or purpose greater than this. If you spend your entire life seeking to love those around you, you will not waste a single moment. Everyone who follows Jesus is equally equipped to love well. You don't have to pursue any special skills to love your neighbor. You can love with extravagance because Jesus' love has set you free.

How can you lay aside the desires of your flesh
in exchange for loving others well?

Received with Gratitude

Since we are surrounded by such a huge cloud of witnesses to the life of faith, let us strip off every weight that slows us down, especially the sin that so easily trips us up. And let us run with endurance the race God has set before us.

HEBREWS 12:1 NLT

Life doesn't always go the way we planned. Seasons change, trials arise, and we compare our path with everyone around us. It's easy to get discouraged and lose our passion for eternity. If we lose sight of the end goal, we will struggle to endure when things are difficult. It's important to remember why we are running. We must keep our eyes steadily fixed upon Jesus if we are going to reach the finish line.

Give your burdens to God and let him strengthen you. When you are tempted to quit running, remember all the people who have gone before you. Let their stories encourage you and give you hope. When you feel you can't go on, look at the countless examples of others. God has faithfully led his people to the finish line for generations.

How can you grow in endurance today?

Reasons to Rejoice

We ought always to give thanks to God for you, brothers and sisters, as is only fitting, because your faith is increasing abundantly, and the love of each and every one of you toward one another grows ever greater.

2 Thessalonians 1:3 nasb

Whatever our purpose in life, we cannot neglect the importance of close relationships. There is so much richness found in friendship and community. There is beauty in sharing our lives with one another. We were not meant to go through this life alone. We honor God when we deliberately grow in love toward each other.

Praise God for the people in your life who are loyal and true friends. You need them, and they are a wonderful gift. Today, search for opportunities to actively grow in love. Look for ways to enrich their lives and encourage them as they walk with the Lord. Put in the work needed to create meaningful connections with the people around you, and you will not be disappointed. Cultivate those relationships with the same tender care that God shows you each day.

*Take time to tell your closest friends
how much they mean to you.*

Yes and Amen

All of God's promises find their "yes" of fulfillment in him.
And as his "yes" and our "amen" ascend to God,
we bring him glory!

2 Corinthians 1:20 TPT

Every promise of God is yes and amen. In other words, every promise will be fulfilled by himself. Every vow he has made will surely come to pass. We can count on it! Along with being our Father, friend, and redeemer, God is our promise keeper. We glorify him by acknowledging his promises and putting our hope in what he has declared.

Your response to God's Word is important. You cannot follow God without agreeing with what he says. An amen should rise from your spirit when you hear his promises. Ask God to align your heart with his and he will do it. He will transform the way you think, and he will show you his perspective. As you fill your life with the knowledge of his Word, you will be encouraged by his faithfulness and reassured of his goodness.

Glorify God today by agreeing with his promises!

December

For everything there is a season,
a time for every activity under heaven.

ECCLESIASTES 3:11 NLT

No Greater Love

"Greater love has no one than this,
than to lay down one's life for his friends.
You are My friends if you do whatever I command you."

JOHN 15:13-14 NKJV

Jesus is our ultimate example of God's love. He showed the greatest love that there is by laying down his life. He gave up everything not only for his friends but for his enemies as well. His love is an open invitation for all to come and find saving grace. Christ's sacrificial love is what saves us, and it serves as an example of how to love others.

Jesus restored your connection with God. He made a way for you to confidently approach your heavenly Father. Love reaches out and considers the needs of others. You can't love someone well without taking notice of what they need. You mirror Christ's love when you sacrifice your time, energy, and resources for the good of those around you.

Today, try to be aware of the needs of those around you.

It All Counts

"There are also many other things that Jesus did, which if they were written one by one, I suppose that even the world itself could not contain the books that would be written."

JOHN 21:25 NCV

Jesus lived for a short thirty-three years on this earth, yet this verse reminds us of the vastness of his influence. He performed countless miracles that weren't recorded in the gospels. What we see in Scripture is only a glimpse of what he did. His actions were a perfect reflection of the Father, and he is still working in the world through his Spirit.

Scripture doesn't hold the fullness of Jesus' work while he was on earth. Every second of his life is not recorded, but you can imagine that it is as rich and God honoring as what you can read. He glorified the Father in every single thing he did. From the moment he woke up, to the moment he went to sleep, God was pleased with him. Remember that your life is also more than the outstanding moments that could be recorded or observed. Every minute of your existence, no matter how mundane, is a testament of God's great love.

How can you glorify God in seemingly unimportant moments?

Keep His Word

"If anyone loves me, he will keep my word.
My Father will love him, and we will come to him
and make our home with him."

JOHN 14:23 CSB

Our claims are empty if we say we follow Jesus but do not keep his commands. Scripture is clear that if we love him, we will do what he says. This would be a stressful task if Jesus were cruel, harsh, or demanding. We know the opposite is true. Everything Jesus instructs us to do is for our good. Listening to him is a delight because his words are always full of life.

If you struggle with the authority of Christ, ask the Holy Spirit to soften your heart. If you let him, he will open your eyes to the great rewards that come from honoring Jesus in all you do. He will steadily guide you toward obedience. Let the Holy Spirit lead you moment by moment, and your days will add up to a lifetime of faithfulness.

How can you honor Jesus today?

Close Contact

Come close to God, and God will come close to you.
Wash your hands, you sinners; purify your hearts,
for your loyalty is divided between God and the world.

JAMES 4:8 NLT

When we draw near to God, he draws near to us. As
soon as we move our hearts toward him, we discover he
is already closer than we realized. Like the father of the
prodigal son, his eye is on us, watching for our return. The
demands of this life are draining, but God's fellowship is
not. It is restorative and kind, life-giving and gentle.

No matter how the world tempts you, you'll never be more
satisfied than you are in God's presence. Remain loyal to the
one who created you and turn away from the ways of the
world. God offers you respite, and he is constantly poised
to help you. Offer your allegiance to the only one who can
give you eternal life in exchange. Draw near to the one who
is always close at hand, for he revives your soul and renews
your hope every time you do.

How can you draw near to God today?

Yielded Hearts

"Father, if you are willing, take this cup from me;
yet not my will, but yours be done."

LUKE 22:42 NIV

It is okay to ask for relief from the things that overwhelm us. There is no benefit to pretending we are strong when we are not. God is not surprised by our weaknesses and limitations. He is not offended by our lack of perseverance or our frustration when challenges arise. Even Jesus asked that the cup of his suffering be taken from him. If Jesus longed for relief, we should not be surprised by our own weariness.

The desire to quit is not the same as quitting. It's normal to want comfort and for your path to be easy. Instead of being discouraged by your weakness, turn it over to God. Pour your heart out to him and let him restore your soul. He will give you strength. He will be with you every step of the way even when you don't think you can go any further. He will never leave you, and he will equip you with grace and mercy as you pursue his will.

Pray honest prayers today and ask for grace to trust God's will.

Build Up

Encourage one another and build one another up,
just as you are doing.

1 THESSALONIANS 5:11 ESV

We need each other. None of us are equipped to walk through life alone. We were created to live in community with other believers. It is good to share our struggles and our successes with people who love us. Loving others is our highest calling. An encouraging word, a selfless deed, or a shoulder to cry on can be the difference between someone persevering and quitting.

Encouragement is a gift to the giver and the recipient. When you take time to strengthen someone else, you will also be refreshed. When your own weaknesses are met with grace, you receive the benefit of being loved well. Lifting each other up in love is a win-win situation. Today, pay attention to the needs of people around you. Surely there is someone in your life who could use an encouraging word.

Ask God to show you someone who needs encouragement.

Holy Helper

"When the Father sends the Advocate as my representative—
that is, the Holy Spirit—he will teach you everything and will
remind you of everything I have told you."

JOHN 14:26 NLT

The Holy Spirit is the greatest gift we have. He is God's
representative in our midst. Until we see God face to face,
the Holy Spirit guides us through life. He helps us and
keeps us steadily walking along a path that honors the Lord.
As we yield to the Spirit's leadership, we find all the wisdom
and encouragement we need. He is more than enough in
every season and situation.

The Holy Spirit is your greatest teacher. He is full of
wisdom, and he reveals God's perspective to you. The Spirit
teaches you to walk in the ways of Christ and to value
the priorities of his kingdom. God knew you would need
help to stay on the right path. He knew that you would
struggle with your weaknesses and shortcomings. The Spirit
reminds you of Christ's teachings and keeps your eyes on
his promises.

How has following the Spirit kept you on the right path?

Easy to Bear

"Simply join your life with mine. Learn my ways and you'll
discover that I'm gentle, humble, easy to please.
You will find refreshment and rest in me.
For all that I require of you will be pleasant and easy to bear."

MATTHEW 11:29-30 TPT

Jesus doesn't require too much from us. He doesn't place
an impossible list of requirements before us, and he doesn't
make it difficult to follow his instructions. He knows what
we are capable of, and he also knows our limits. When we
turn to him, he meets us with overwhelming grace and
mercy. His love meets all our needs, and he offers rest for
our weary souls.

Listen to Jesus' invitation and respond wholeheartedly.
Hear the compassion and kindness in his voice and let
his love wash over you. He sees you, knows you, and calls
you his own. He knows your struggles, yet he offers you
peace and strength. Join your life to his and you won't be
disappointed.

*It is never too late to take Jesus up on his invitation
for rest and refreshment.*

Strong Tower

The name of the LORD is a strong tower;
The righteous run to it and are safe.

PROVERBS 18:10 NKJV

When the world is falling apart, we don't have to despair.
There is refuge for our souls in the name of the Lord. He
surrounds us with his presence, and he fills us with courage.
The name of the Lord is a strong tower, and we are safe
when we call upon him.

Proverbs says that the righteous run to the Lord and are
safe. This insinuates that action is required on your part.
When fear overwhelms you, turn to the Lord. Posture
your heart before him and acknowledge your need for his
protection. Run to him and trust that he will receive you
with open arms. He will not turn you away when you need
help. He is ready and waiting to bear your burdens and
protect you from harm.

Call on the name of the Lord when you need him today.

Healing Hope

Confess your sins to each other
and pray for each other so God can heal you.
When a believing person prays, great things happen.

JAMES 5:16 NCV

When we are honest about our failures, we can pray for each other, offer compassion, and find encouragement. It is empowering to share the reality of our lives with each other and realize we aren't alone. When we are vulnerable about our shortcomings, we make space for others to also confess their sins and find freedom.

What keeps you from confessing your sins? Are you afraid you're the only one who struggles with your particular issue? Are you worried about what others will think of you? Projecting a picture-perfect version of your life won't cultivate intimacy or authenticity in your relationships. Ask God to show you someone in your life who is trustworthy. As you openly talk about the negative parts of your life, you'll find freedom and abundant grace.

*How has being open about your sins
had a positive impact on your life?*

Take a Break

In vain you get up early and stay up late,
working hard to have enough food—
yes, he gives sleep to the one he loves.

PSALM 127:2 CSB

We are not meant to work ourselves into exhaustion. It is good to have a strong work ethic, but it is also good to know how to rest properly. The pursuit of money is not supposed to be our top priority. While our culture says that we should always be hustling for the next thing, God says that we should trust him to provide for us.

Consistent anxiety over your finances isn't sustainable. Your health, both mental and physical, will suffer. If you are worried about practical needs in your life, ask God for guidance. He will give you wisdom to make decisions and peace to calm your weary heart. Let him grant you rest for your body and soul. Lay your burdens at his feet and he will faithfully take care of you.

Ask the Holy Spirit how you can embrace the practice of rest.

Daily Encouragement

Encourage one another daily, as long as it is called "Today," so that none of you may be hardened by sin's deceitfulness.

HEBREWS 3:13 NIV

Our words have the power to lift up those who are down. We can encourage our fellow believers to have endurance and stay on the path of righteousness. We have the opportunity to infuse hope, courage, and peace into the people around us. When the hardships of life are too much to bear, we bear one another's burdens. This is the beauty of community.

God designed you to need other people. You aren't meant to walk through life alone. The encouragement and companionship of other people is necessary. You need others to lift you up and to lovingly help you overcome temptation and sin. If you lack community, ask God to bring other believers into your life. He knows what you need, and he is happy to provide for you.

Who can you encourage today?

Wonderfully Complex

Thank you for making me so wonderfully complex!
Your workmanship is marvelous—how well I know it.

PSALM 139:14 NLT

The complex parts of us may seem difficult to understand, but they are not unknown to the one who stitched us together. He knew what he was doing when he made each of us. As our maker, he doesn't have to work to understand us. He knows our talents, weaknesses, thoughts, and intentions. Nothing about us is hidden from his sight.

You were made by the Creator of all good things. He made you with intention and creativity. You are unique, and you reflect the wonderful goodness of the God who made you. Regardless of how you perceive yourself, God sees you with mercy and delight. Your existence glorifies God and brings him joy.

Ask God to give you confidence in his perspective of you.

Past Principles

Whatever was written in former days was written for our instruction, that through endurance and through the encouragement of the Scriptures we might have hope.

ROMANS 15:4 ESV

While it is good to look ahead to new opportunities, it is also important to learn from what has already happened. If we honor the lessons of the past, we can readily move into the future with wisdom. We find hope and encouragement when we look at how God has already been faithful. The realization that he has kept so many promises reassures us that he will continue to do so.

God is steady and consistent. He will not let you down. From your first breath until your last, God is your sustainer. Look at all the ways he has shown up in your life. Think about how he has kept you safe, encouraged you, and blessed you with his presence. Let those memories spur you on to endurance and faithfulness.

How does your past encourage you to endure the future?

Joy in the Journey

Consider it all joy, my brothers and sisters, when you encounter various trials, knowing that the testing of your faith produces endurance. And let endurance have its perfect result, so that you may be perfect and complete, lacking in nothing.

JAMES 1:2-4 NASB

No matter what we go through, there is reason to rejoice! God is always read to help, encourage, and guide us. He teaches us to make the right decisions, and he comforts us when we fall. He is all that we need. He is able to take our worst days and use them to strengthen our character. Even when we can't see a purpose for our pain, God is continually working in our lives.

You get to decide how you perceive the difficulties in your life. You can see them as an opportunity to lean on the Lord and be strengthened, or you can look at them and be discouraged and overwhelmed. God is capable of producing endurance and faithfulness in your life. He is not finished with you yet.

Rejoice that even miserable circumstances can be used for your good.

Grace Gifts

If your gift is to encourage others, be encouraging. If it is giving, give generously. If God has given you leadership ability, take the responsibility seriously. And if you have a gift for showing kindness to others, do it gladly.

ROMANS 12:8 NLT

God has given each of us different gifts. No matter how they play out, they all have the same purpose. We are meant to use them for the benefit of other people. It pleases God when we use our gifts in service to each other. As we rely on each other, we are stronger than when we are alone. This is why it is worth our time and effort to develop and hone our gifts.

You have been given specific gifts. Ask the Holy Spirit to show you what they are. As your eyes are opened, you can focus on how God has blessed you. Don't worry about areas that don't appeal to you or aren't natural for you. Instead, take notice of how God made you and seek to be strengthened in those areas.

Use your gifts to serve someone today.

Turn Your Attention

I have set the LORD always before me;
Because He is at my right hand I shall not be moved.

PSALM 16:8 NKJV

It is good to posture ourselves before the Lord. When we turn our hearts and minds toward him, we set ourselves up to receive everything he offers us. As we turn away from distractions and frustrations, we acknowledge that God is present and worthy of our praise. We intentionally turn our attention to God, and he faithfully meets us every time.

There are many ways you can set the Lord before you. Time spent reading the Word, in worship, and in prayer, can bolster your hope and keep your heart turned toward God. Little habits will add up to a lifetime of mindfully acknowledging him. As you practice creating an environment of continual worship in your life, you'll reap the rewards of carrying God's presence with you everywhere you go.

As many times as you think of it to today,
turn your attention to God.

Communal Support

Let us consider one another in order to provoke love and good works, not neglecting to gather together, as some are in the habit of doing, but encouraging each other, and all the more as you see the day approaching.

HEBREWS 10:24-25 CSB

We all need community. If we try navigating life alone, we will eventually succumb to our own weaknesses. We all struggle and fall short of the glory of God. This is not a formal accusation against our character, rather it is the reality of our human condition. We need the encouragement, accountability, and wisdom of others. Giving and receiving support is one way we can keep our hope alive as we wait for Christ's return.

You need a reliable support system. You aren't meant to shoulder every burden in your life alone. There is so much value in being able to give and receive support. If you feel lonely, ask God to highlight a few relationships you can depend on. He knows what you need, and he is happy to provide for you.

Thank God for the community you have and ask him for what you need.

Practice Peace

Let us try to do what makes peace
and helps one another.

ROMANS 14:19 NCV

We live in a culture that loves dissention. We love arguments, passionate opinions, and picking sides. While it's normal to disagree, the pursuit of peace should not take a back seat to our personal perspectives. No matter what we think about an issue, we should always prioritize speaking and acting in a way that promotes peace. Above all else, we are called to love our neighbor.

There will be times when the pursuit of peace means staying quiet. There will be other times when it means speaking clearly, definitively, and without fear. If you let him, the Holy Spirit will give you discernment to know the difference between both situations. As you follow him, he will fill you with gentleness, peace, and wisdom. Instead of letting your own passions rule your interactions, you'll create life-giving connections by building others up.

How can you practice peace in your relationships today?

Take Heart

Be strong and courageous,
all you who put your hope in the LORD!

PSALM 31:24 NLT

David, the author of Psalm 31, didn't diminish his needs when he called out to the Lord. He didn't act like there wasn't a problem or that everything was completely fine. His pleas did not come at the end of an ordinary day. He was in the middle of great trials and tribulations. Amidst his pain, he commanded his soul to be strong and courageous.

When it feels like your whole world is shaking, call upon the Lord. Tell your soul to rise up and be strong. Your hope doesn't come from your ability to handle your situation. Instead, it comes from knowing that God's strength is more than enough. You can courageously approach whatever you are facing because you know God is on your side. Take heart, strengthen your resolve, and remember you are never alone.

*Let God's faithfulness strengthen you
as you continue to trust him.*

Helping Hand

"I am the LORD your God
who takes hold of your right hand
and says to you, Do not fear;
I will help you."

ISAIAH 41:13 NIV

Our heavenly Father is gracious and kind. As his children, we depend on his leadership. A good parent is always ready to offer their hand whenever their child needs it. They don't observe difficulty and refuse to help. A good parent knows exactly when and how to step in. God does the same with us. When we struggle, he reaches out with strength and love.

Today, God is telling you to set your fears aside. He is calling you to trust in him and to believe that he will help you in your time of need. As you reach out to him, he takes hold of your hand and stays close. However your day unfolds, he will never forsake you. Take his words to heart and be reassured of his faithfulness.

What fears can you lay aside today?

Firm Foundation

The Lord is faithful.
He will establish you and guard you
against the evil one.

2 THESSALONIANS 3:3 ESV

God keeps his promises. He doesn't always work in ways we expect, but that does not diminish his faithfulness. We don't see everything clearly, and we miss the details he considers. Whatever our own expectations, we can trust his faithful love to stand the test of time. We can firmly believe that he will do what he says.

As you trust in him, God promises to establish you. He will set your feet upon a rock, and he will keep you steady no matter what comes your way. Your soul is secure in his love, and you cannot be snatched out of his hands. You are his beloved child, and he will keep you safe. Nothing can come against you when he is your protector.

How has God been faithful to you?

Humble and Lowly

"Do not be afraid, Mary, for you have found favor with God. And behold, you will conceive in your womb and give birth to a son, and you shall name Him Jesus."

LUKE 1:30-31 NASB

When the angel appeared to Mary, she was nobody special in the eyes of anyone around her. She didn't stand out because of stature or fame. She was just a teenager, and she lived a quiet and humble life. Still, the God of the universe chose her to be the mother of Jesus. She found favor with God, and he honored her in an incredible way.

If we use worldly standards of success, each scriptural account of great faith would miss the mark. God rarely chose the strong, wise, wealthy, and well-known to accomplish his will. Instead, he focused on those who were lowly, humble, and willing. Be encouraged by God's definition of success. Surely, he will do good things in and through your life.

How have you seen God's favor in your life?

God With Us

"Listen! A virgin will be pregnant,
she will give birth to a Son,
and he will be known as 'Emmanuel,'
which means in Hebrew, 'God became one of us.'"

MATTHEW 1:23 TPT

Jesus' birth was prophesied long before Mary carried him. Since Adam and Eve left the garden, humanity has been longing for a savior. After thousands of years of prophecies, Jesus walked the earth and showed us the way to the Father. He became one of us. He didn't sit at the height of the heavens and shout commands. He knelt down, got on our level, and lovingly offered us redemption.

Jesus is your great advocate. He put on flesh and bones, and he experienced all the limitations of being human. In him, you have a leader who can relate to the weakness you experience. He is not far away, unfeeling, or irrelevant. He understands your pain and vulnerability more than you realize. Today, find comfort in the very near presence of Christ.

How can you embrace Jesus as Emmanuel this season?

Worthy Gifts

When they had come into the house, they saw the young
Child with Mary His mother, and fell down and worshiped
Him. And when they had opened their treasures, they
presented gifts to Him: gold, frankincense, and myrrh.

MATTHEW 2:11 NKJV

Jesus' birth was a celebration. Though few on earth knew
the long-awaited Messiah had arrived, God made sure
that there was still a commemoration of this momentous
occasion! Just as an angel had appeared to Mary to
inform her of her coming conception, so angels informed
shepherds and wise men of Jesus' birth and its significance.

The wise men followed the rising star all the way to the
Christ child. They brought him gifts of gold, frankincense,
and myrrh. These were costly gifts that would normally be
given to a king. The wise men knew Jesus would be king of
the Jews, and they came with gifts to honor him rightly. As
you celebrate Christ's birth, you also can present him with
gifts to honor him. He is worthy of your praise and daily
devotion.

*Give God a gift that costs you something today—
this can include your time or your attention.*

Our High Priest

Without doubt, the secret of our life of worship is great:
He was shown to us in a human body,
proved right in spirit, and seen by angels.
He was proclaimed to the nations,
believed in by the world, and taken up in glory.

1 TIMOTHY 3:16 NCV

Jesus is worthy of our worship. We offer our lives to him because of who he is and what he has done. He left the perfection of heaven to walk the earth and redeem the lost. Everything he did was perfect. He gave us a glimpse of what the Father is like, and he showed us the way to eternity in his presence.

Everything you need can be found in Jesus. He is your great high priest who intercedes on your behalf. He is your righteousness, and he is your way to the Father. He is at the center of your faith and is the motivation for everything you believe in. He is your great hope and the source of your salvation. He laid down his life for you, and he is worthy of praise.

How can you offer praise to Jesus today?

Search Me

Search me, God, and know my heart;
test me and know my concerns.
See if there is any offensive way in me;
lead me in the everlasting way.

PSALM 139:23-24 CSB

When we give the God access to search our hearts, we open ourselves to his correction, wisdom, and leadership. Our invitation to search and test our hearts is an act of worship. It's an acknowledgment that his ways are higher than ours. We willingly grant him access to our innermost thoughts because we know he is gentle, kind, and full of love.

Offer your heart to God without fear or shame. He knows every part of you, and he is not disappointed in you. When he highlights an area that needs transformation, he does it with kindness. He is never harsh, critical, or unforgiving. He has your best in mind, and he desires health and wholeness for you. He wants to lead you on the path to everlasting life. Trust his direction and submit to his servant-hearted leadership.

*What holds you back from inviting God
into the deepest parts of your heart?*

Secrets of God

It was to us that God revealed these things by his Spirit.
For his Spirit searches out everything
and shows us God's deep secrets.

1 CORINTHIANS 2:10 NLT

God wants us to experience his goodness. He wants to
be known by us. God has given us his Spirit to reveal the
secrets of his kingdom. The Spirit knows the depths of who
God is, and he freely shares with us. The ways of God are
no longer a secret. He isn't hiding from us, and we don't
have to guess what he is like. Through the Spirit, we have
fellowship with him.

God has good things in store for you. He wants you to
experience the wonders of his presence for all eternity. Follow
him and you will not be disappointed. His love is better than
you can imagine, and he offers it to you without limitations.
Today, ask the Holy Spirit to reveal God's heart to you. As you
seek him, you will find what you are looking for.

*Connect with the Spirit today, allowing him
to reveal the wonders of God.*

Loving Counsel

"I will instruct you and teach you in the way you should go;
I will counsel you with my loving eye on you."

PSALM 32:8 NIV

When we dream about the future, we must remember God is with us every step of the way. No matter what are hopes and plans are, God is already aware of the details of our lives. There isn't anything that surprises him. We set ourselves up for success when we submit to his ways and commit our plans to him. He faithfully instructs us, and he counsels us with love.

As you prepare for the new year, don't forget God is your greatest source of wisdom. Apart from him, every lofty goal or meticulous plan falls flat. He knows the best path forward, and he already sees the obstacles in your way. Lean into his presence and trust him to guide you. Follow his lead, and he will instruct you in the way you should go.

Ask God to lead you and trust in his instruction.

Citizens of Heaven

Our citizenship is in heaven, and from it we await a Savior, the Lord Jesus Christ, who will transform our lowly body to be like his glorious body, by the power that enables him even to subject all things to himself.

PHILIPPIANS 3:20-21 ESV

Our hope isn't found in what we can see or experience. We press on through the challenges of this life because our hope lies in eternity spent with God. Our true citizenship, our rightful belonging, is found in heaven. While the world may seem hopeless and corrupt, our faith is not shaken because we know we don't belong here.

Keep your heart rooted in eternity. The nations of this earth rise and fall, but they are not where you plant your flag. The kingdom of Christ is better than anything you have known in this world. When you are tempted to give your allegiance to people or powers of the world, choose the way of Christ instead. He is your king and your true hope.

How can you be sure your hope doesn't rely on the success of worldly systems or authorities?

Don't Give Up

Let this hope burst forth within you,
releasing a continual joy.
Don't give up in a time of trouble,
but commune with God at all times.

ROMANS 12:12 TPT

As long as there is breath in our lungs, there is hope. There is joy available in communion with the Lord. There is continual grace flowing from the throne of your loving Father to each of us. This is always true. The circumstances of our lives cannot diminish his faithfulness. In times of trouble God is near.

Have you experienced trouble over the last year? Notice how God has sustained you and brought you to the other side of it. Praise him for all he's done. Allow hope to grow within you as you dwell on God's good works. If you are still in the middle of a trial remember that God is with you. He will never leave you or forsake you. He is faithful to those who follow him.

Thank God for how he has carried you
through each of your days.